Breaking Free from Sin's Grip

BREAKING FREE FROM SIN'S GRIP

HOLINESS DEFINED FOR A NEW GENERATION

FRANK MOORE

Beacon Hill Press of Kansas City
Kansas City, Missouri

Copyright 2001
by Beacon Hill Press of Kansas City

ISBN 083-411-8920

Printed in the
United States of America

Cover Design: Kevin Williamson

Library of Congress Cataloging-in-Publication Data

Moore, Frank, 1951-
  Breaking free from sin's grip : holiness defined for a new generation / Frank Moore.
     p. cm.
  Includes bibliographical references.
  ISBN 0-8341-1892-0 (pbk.)
   1. Holiness 2. Holiness—Biblical teaching. I. Title.

 BT767 .M67 2001
 234'.8—dc21

2001018443

10   9   8   7   6   5   4   3

Dedicated to my students
ministering around the world
who are sharing the message
of full salvation

Contents

There are times when
parenthood seems nothing
but feeding the mouth
that bites you.
—*Peter De Vries*[1]

1

AN ADVENTURE STORY

The Bag Lady

She passed in front of our Cincinnati home every day, usually about midmorning. I didn't know exactly what time of the day she'd scuff down the sidewalk, but I always knew what she'd be wearing: no matter what time of year, or what the weather, she'd wear a black wool coat buttoned all the way to her neck. And she always carried a big paper bag with plastic handles, the kind you get at the entrance of a mall department store. She walked by our house picking up stray paper, cans, and bottles, and putting them in her paper sack.

She lived just around the corner from our house. I had a clear view of her backyard from my front yard. None of the neighbors knew much about the little old lady. She never talked to any of us, and she always kept her house window shades pulled. I guess you might call her a mystery lady who lived a very private life.

> *A scene of shock and horror greeted the policemen as they stepped into the house.*

I wondered about her occasionally as she passed in front of our house but wrote her off as an eccentric old woman who marched to the beat of a different drummer—a very different drummer!

One warm, summer day she missed her walk. Another day passed. When the third day came and went without her regular stroll through the neighborhood, the neighbors worried. They called the police. When the policemen knocked on the lady's door and received no response, they broke the door in.

A scene of shock and horror greeted the policemen as they stepped into the house. From floor to ceiling in the living room, like some bizarre art form, were stacked the stray paper, cans, and bottles from the lady's daily walks.

A narrow, tunnel-like path led from the living room to the dining room where they found the same type of junk collection. The path to the front bedroom yielded even more. Every room was completely filled, floor to ceiling, with garbage. When the policemen reached the back bedroom of the house, they found the old woman dead in her bed.

The police called the county coroner to take the lady's body away.

Our little old trash-collecting neighbor had lived in dire poverty with nearly $2 million cash at her fingertips.

The next day a semi delivered a large Dumpster to the driveway for the garbage. Yellow tape outlined the entire property making it off-limits to all of us. The police began hauling the refuse from the house to the Dumpster with wheelbarrows. When they dug their way down to the couch, they noticed the couch pillow appeared rather lumpy, so they unzipped it. Much to their surprise, they found the pillowcase filled, not with cotton stuffing, but with money. A second lumpy pillow guarded the same treasure. So did the third. Their interest now piqued, they searched the couch cushions.

You guessed it—all the pillows served as safe-deposit boxes for large sums of money. Now the police took an entirely new interest in their room-by-room cleanup of the house. Nearly every room had drawers or pillows stuffed with cash. The back bedroom contained the mother lode, with the largest jackpot found in the bed pillows and mattress.

When the garbage was all sorted and loaded into the Dumpster, and the money all stacked and counted, the police determined that our little old trash-collecting neighbor had lived in dire poverty with nearly $2 million cash at her fingertips.

Living as if We're on Our Own

I've often thought of that lady's circumstance and wondered if it is similar to some of our circumstances on the Christian path. So often I hear Christians talk about how hard they find it to live admirably or resist temptation or remain consistent, or control emotions and reactions. I hear the struggle of living in this fallen world described in vivid detail and sympathize with the plight. We do live in hostile territory—trying to live righteously in an unrighteous world, trying to honor God in a world that doesn't make a place for Him.

However, I also know God provides indescribable resources for victorious living at our fingertips. We don't always remember His ample provisions, though. My bag lady neighbor reminds me of our tendency in Christian circles to live with the presence and power of God all around us yet respond to spiritual needs as though we are completely on our own. That's never the case; we're never on our own. A loving Heavenly Father involves himself in our lives in the most intimate ways. His personal involvement is incredibly special.

A Special Night

A half dozen events hold a special place in my life. One of those events began in the middle of the night when my wife, Sue, awakened me, announcing the time had arrived to take her to the hospital to give birth to our child. All our anxious anticipation over several months had pointed to this moment.

Words mock my attempt to capture the flood of emotion that washed over me as I held Brent in my arms for the first time.

The wake-up call came several weeks early, so neither of us expected it. We hurriedly loaded the car and headed toward the hospital, 75 miles away. Nature moved faster than our speeding vehicle, so we welcomed the state police officer's red and blue flashing lights as he pulled us over to the side of the road with the news that an ambulance was on the way.

Our journey soon continued at an even faster pace in the ambulance. Paramedics worked with Sue, while the driver and I talked with the doctor on the radio. Should we continue to try and reach the hospital or pull over to the side of the road and deliver our child in the ambulance?

As each mile passed, we reevaluated the decision to continue. We contacted another nearby hospital, but they had no delivery staff on duty. So, we continued toward our destination. We finally made it—not a minute too soon! Nurses raced Sue directly to the delivery room where a staff of experts waited, prepped and ready. I hurried to the hospital's Admitting Office. I had just finished signing the admission papers when Sue and our new son rolled out of the delivery room to greet me.

Words mock my attempt to capture the flood of emotion that washed over me as I held Brent in my arms for the first time. I began talking to him like I would talk to a longlost friend. In a single moment, all my hopes and dreams for his lifetime flashed across the screen of my mind. I assured him I would love and care for him as long as I lived. I told him all the things we would do when he got old enough. I promised him I would be the best dad I could be. What a sacred time we had together, an awesome memory to this very day!

Our Heavenly Father's Hopes and Dreams

I often think of the way I felt as I held Brent that day. I recall all my hopes and dreams for his life. I wonder how God felt as He pondered the creation of His children Adam and Eve for the first time? I wonder what hopes and dreams for their lives ran through His mind? I wonder what parental plans He laid for them? I wonder what promises He made to them when He looked at them for the first time? No doubt those moments were even more special to God than my moments with Brent were to me.

We're exploring a story, really. An adventure story.

The Bible points out that our holy God created us in His image (Gen. 1:26-27). Since we are like God in many ways, we can look at our lives and relationships and learn a great deal about God and the way He wants to relate to us. God does not want us to play guessing games to try and figure out who He is, what He is like, what pleases Him, and how we can live in relationship with Him.

He reveals himself to us in a variety of ways to answer all of these questions plainly. Through creation, through historical events in the world, through circumstances in our personal lives, through the life and ministry of Jesus Christ, through the Bible, and through our own psychological, emotional, and social makeup, God speaks volumes about himself and His incredible plan for us.

We're exploring a story, really. An adventure story. It has highs and lows, mystery and suspense, glorious moments and times of sorrow and despair. The story is still being written, so it doesn't have an end yet—though the Bible paints a pretty clear picture of how it will conclude someday. It's much like any story of the parent/child relationship. The main characters of this adventure story are God and humanity.

The Book Layout

In this book, we'll explore the features of that story again, from the Father's perspective. Like any good parent He had a lifetime of hopes and dreams for His children. Like many parental plans, they didn't always turn out like He'd hoped. Like the quote at the beginning of this chapter, God tried to feed us; we bit Him. But He didn't throw in the towel and quit. He came back again and again with new enthusiasm to refocus His plans into reality for His children.

This is not a story from long ago; it's as current as this morning's coffee. It's not a story about someone else, somewhere else; it's about you and me right where we live today. That's what holds our interest—we're the main characters. We're not going to look through a window into someone else's world to explore this story; we're going to look into a mirror at our own world.

We'll first look at the Father's plan for His children. Then we'll see how we derailed that plan and took it into an entirely different direction. We'll explore the ways the Father involved himself in our lives and sought to bring us back to His original plan for us. We will especially emphasize how our actions and responses to the Father's offers figure into this picture and what the Father does to bring His hopes and dreams for us to reality.

Sometimes we get busy trying to make it through a rough day. We just want to make ends meet or try to make the best of a bad situation. We get so occupied that we forget about this intersection of the Father's hopes and dreams for us, and our own desire to have things turn out right.

We spoke earlier about how hard some folks find it to live admirably or resist temptation or remain consistent or control emotions and reactions. Our struggles are not unrelated to God's best wishes for us. They vitally connect. Our attempts to live righteously in an unrighteous world —to honor God in a world that doesn't make a place for Him—do not go unnoticed by God. He sees our good desires and stands ready to help.

God knows right where to locate those best desires because He placed them in us on creation day. Moreover, He works in unexplainable ways to give us hope where we see no hope. And He works circumstances together to reach positive ends far beyond our wildest dreams.

He doesn't do this because He feels sorry for us or because we beg for His help. Rather, it's all part of His parental visions He had for us back in the Garden of Eden when He first laid eyes on us and said, "Awesome!" (my interpretation of "very good").

This story will eventually lead to the notion of a biblical concept of holiness. Actually, the whole story relates to holiness in one way or another. Just saying the word *holiness* scares some people. It really shouldn't scare us, however. Holiness is not an abstract concept, a theory to be proved, or a doctrine to be dissected. Neither is it an argument that's won by stringing a whole ream of Bible verses together.

Holiness describes a way of living made possible through intimate personal relationship with God. Holiness speaks of life and relationship, not letter and law, not doctrine and theory. And that changes our discussion's complexion. So, when we explore this awesome adventure story of God and us, we'll want to learn all we can about holiness as well.

Holiness discussions scare folks because an entire vocabulary has sprung up around previous arguments over the years. Many new words emerged in the process. Some of these words have similar meanings. Yet, boatloads of effort have been expended to distinguish between them. Occasionally, the meanings have about a hair's width of distance between them, requiring a microscope and tweezers to separate them. Sometimes the distinctions matter; sometimes they don't. Either way, such words scare people.

So, for the most part, we'll avoid using such words. We'll use biblical words not abstract ones. We'll attempt to tell this amazing adventure story about God and humanity without getting caught up in the tornado swirl of abstract concepts and theological jargon.

Don't get me wrong. Abstract concepts and theological language are neither bad nor meaningless. They provide important analysis and reflection. However, most people do not connect with them in ways that add value to their lives or understanding to their faith.

The concepts and language do have value, though. It's like the freshly picked ears of corn from our farm. When you stand in our cornfield and pull a ripe ear of corn from the stalk, you don't know what you're getting. You only see the green wrap of shucks. After you peel the shucks away and pull off all the silk threads, you begin to see the beautiful kernels of corn.

Those abstract concepts and theological words resemble the freshly picked ear of corn. When you look beneath them, you begin to see the beautiful experience believers enjoy with God. As these believers share together with one another about how God works in their lives, they find points of connection with their experiences.

God works similarly with His children. So, they coin words and concepts to capture these experiences. These words and concepts, like photos in a family album, tell the story of God's workings in His children's lives. We'll attempt to get behind these words and concepts to take a fresh look at the adventure story that prompted them in the first place.

So, that's where we'll go from here: back to a Father seeing His children for the first time and dreaming big dreams for them. Then we'll head down through the valley of sorrow as His children reject those dreams. From there we'll climb back up the mountain of hope as He devises a plan to recapture the dreams and turn them into realities for all who let Him. I know this wonderful story will interest you. After all, you're in it!

Fast Takes

1. It is possible for us to struggle in our Christian walk unnecessarily because God provides indescribable resources for victorious living at our fingertips.

2. God has hopes and dreams for His children just as we have hopes and dreams for our children.

3. We're main characters in God's incredible adventure story.

4. God wants to help us more than we even want His help.

5. Holiness is life and relationship with God.

Think About This . . .

1. What do you think are the biggest misconceptions about holiness?

2. Why do members of holiness churches have such a hard time explaining the concept of holiness to others?

3. Why do you think holiness is so hard for people to understand?

4. Parents, describe the way you felt when you held your firstborn in your arms for the first time. Relate your emotions to the way God felt when He created humanity.

5. What dreams and plans did you have for your children when they were born? Relate your dreams and plans for your children to God's dreams and plans for His children.

6. Describe how God planned everything to be for His children in the Garden of Eden.

7. Discuss ways we learn about God through creation, through historical events in the world or in our personal lives, through the life and ministry of Jesus Christ, through the Bible, and through our own psychological, emotional, and social makeup.

It wasn't an apple from
the tree that started the
trouble in the Garden of
Eden; it was the pair on
the ground.

2

THE TEST

Created on Purpose

The Book of Genesis begins the story of humanity at the very beginning: Day 1 of everything on earth. We see God creating all reality and humanity on purpose. We're no accident of nature. We cannot trace our heritage back to the jungle or to the one-celled green sludge floating on the pond. God directly created us. Although we have a physical body like the animals, we are different in important ways.

One of our most significant differences from animals exists because God made us for personal fellowship with himself and each other. He put something of himself in us, for He made us in His image. Having God's image means we also possess many characteristics, such as self-awareness, imagination, use of complex language, communion with God, self-direction, ability to think philosophically, creativity, capacity for memories, and a never-dying soul.

Our Father placed us in a picture-postcard paradise and said, "Enjoy." Every pleasure waited at our fingertips. He then stepped back, looked at the whole scene from a panoramic view, and declared it all "very good" (Gen. 1:31). He envisioned an incredible parental plan and brought it into being. What a sense of fulfillment! What a father's joy!

Holy God; Holy Children

In various ways, God reminds us throughout His Word that He is holy and that His hopes and dreams for us include our also being holy. That has been His plan from the first days in the garden. He wants a great life for us. He wants us to know only joy without heartache. He wants us to love and care for each other. He wants us to do right. He wants us to live by the Golden Rule as we prefer the needs of others above our own. He wants us to avoid the pain and scars of sin. He wants to save us from the negative consequences of disobeying Him.

As a parent, God has our best interest in mind. He wants us to find untarnished fulfillment in daily living. He knows the only way for His plan to work in our lives is for us to participate in His plan for our holiness.

The only way for His plan to work in our lives is for us to participate in His plan for our holiness.

So, He started us in the picture-perfect garden setting. Our holy God not only placed us in a perfect environment but also gave us a holy, innocent heart. We did not start life in a neutral position, like sitting on a fence between the fields of good and evil. No, He planted our feet firmly in the field of good. Like well-protected infants, we knew no wrong. We knew only God and the good He placed around us. He gave us an inner urge to love and please Him. We lived close to Him as we took daily garden walks with Him in the cool of the afternoon.

Wired for Him

God wired us for himself much like a computer gets wired to be a home computer. When you buy a computer at the electronics store, bring it home, take it out of the box, plug it into the electrical socket, and turn it on, it responds as a home computer because it was programmed at the factory to respond that way. Though it has many of the same electronic components as a car's dashboard, an elevator's operation hardware, or a missile's guidance system, it is none of these things. It is configured to be a home computer, and it works best only when used in that way.

Just so, God created us to live our lives with Him at the center of our existence. We can place cars, houses, boats, careers, travel, pleasure, fame, money, or anything else at the center of our existence if we choose to do so. A lot of folks do. However, if we do this, the pieces of life's puzzle will never fit together properly. We'll sense a misfit. Why? Because God made us for himself and placed an empty spot at the center of our being that only He can fill. Without Him in the center spot of our lives, life never makes sense. We become spiritually, emotionally, and psychologically crippled and deformed when we leave God out of our lives and thus alienate ourselves from our created purpose.

God's Big Limitation

We cannot complete a description of God's creation of us without talking about a very important limitation God placed upon himself. We speak often of God's all-powerfulness. We like to think He does anything He wants to do at any time He wants to do it. We like to think of God as stronger than anyone else in the universe, similar to the way we compared our fathers to our friends' fathers on the elementary school playground. You know: "My dad is stronger than your dad." This is usually true of God, but not always.

God flung a million stars in the sky across a million miles; they fell into place, and they shine just as He planned for them to shine. He created planets beyond our wildest imagination and set them in motion in galaxies that reach beyond our loftiest thoughts and strongest telescopes—they rotate and interact with one another just as He planned for them to do. He created plant life, animal life, and sea life both large and small and placed them in their respective environments—they live and function and reproduce just as He planned for them to do.

Then, this all-powerful God carefully crafted humanity, but with a very different quality from the rest of His creation. He gave us life, movement, and a purpose like the rest of creation. But He also gave us a very powerful tool for both good and evil. We call it free will.

> *With this free will we can choose to love and obey Him, or we can choose to break His heart.*

With this free will we can choose to love and obey Him, or we can choose to break His heart. Why would this all-powerful God give us such a wonderful and terrible ability? Why so much potential for both good and evil in the same gift? Because He wants us to love and obey Him freely, not because we are programmed from the factory to do so.

A home computer doesn't have a choice; it must respond as a home computer. We have a choice; we're not robots. That's the only way love can be true love and obedience true obedience.

Think about it for a minute. What if your mate or best friend told you he or she loved you every day for many years. Then, you accidentally opened that person's mail one day and found a check from your mother. Your mother was paying that person to tell you he or she loved you! You wouldn't feel the love was genuine, would you?

What kind of love and obedience would we give God if we were programmed to do so? Not very meaningful, right? That's the reason for free will.

Now, God knew our free will came packaged with a risk. No money-back guarantees here. Free will could be a double-edged sword. We could freely choose to love and obey Him, or we could freely choose to reject Him and break His heart. That was a risk God willingly took because the reward of genuine love and obedience was so great. Like any good parent, God placed His children in the best possible environment. He explained the ground rules for living life, established meaningful relationship with daily afternoon walks, and then backed off to give humanity the space in which to use their freedom. As we do with wobbly toddlers, God took His hands away and hoped we would choose to walk in a morally straight line.

The Test

Why did God give us this space? Because our desires and affections required testing. We knew what God wanted, but would we choose to do it of our own free will? Only a test would reveal the answer.

Take, for example, our love relationships. Junior high school boys and girls fall in and out of love almost as often as the wind changes direction. Junior high school teachers need a score card to keep up with the romances on any given day. These relationships usually cannot pass the test of the next cute guy or gal walking down the hall. Affections quickly shift to the next conquest. A tested love, on the other hand, is the love a husband has for his wife or the love a wife has for her husband across a lifetime of choices and temptations. That kind of tested love proves true love.

So, back to the garden and the test. You know the story well; it's recorded in the Book of Genesis.

Now the serpent was more crafty than any of the wild animals the LORD God had made. He said to the woman, "Did God really say, 'You must not eat from any tree in the garden'?"

The woman said to the serpent, "We may eat fruit from the trees in the garden, but God did say, 'You must not eat fruit from the tree that is in the middle of the garden, and you must not touch it, or you will die.'"

"You will not surely die," the serpent said to the woman. "For God knows that when you eat of it your eyes will be opened, and you will be like God, knowing good and evil."

When the woman saw that the fruit of the tree was good for food and pleasing to the eye, and also desirable for gaining wisdom, she took some and ate it. She also gave some to her husband, who was with her, and he ate it. Then the eyes of both of them were opened, and they realized they were naked; so they sewed fig leaves together and made coverings for themselves.

Then the man and his wife heard the sound of the LORD God as he was walking in the garden in the cool of the day, and they hid from the LORD God among the trees of the garden. But the LORD God called to the man, "Where are you?"

He answered, "I heard you in the garden, and I was afraid because I was naked; so I hid."

And he said, "Who told you that you were naked? Have you eaten from the tree that I commanded you not to eat from?"

The man said, "The woman you put here with me—she gave me some fruit from the tree, and I ate it."

Then the LORD God said to the woman, "What is this you have done?"

The woman said, "The serpent deceived me, and I ate" *(Gen. 3:1-13).*

Free will exercised; God disobeyed; blame passed. And we thought blaming others for our problems started recently! Bern Williams said, "If Adam and Eve were alive today, they would probably sue the snake."[1]

> *We decided we would do what we wanted to do, and we would do it our way.*

It certainly is a good thing television and talk shows hadn't been invented yet. I can see it now. Adam, Eve, and the serpent all occupying chairs at the center of the studio stage and each waving their arms, shouting at each other, and blaming other people for their wrong choices.

Adam blamed Eve; Eve blamed the serpent; the serpent blamed God. Interpret the situation any way you like. It boils down to this: given the option of self-sovereignty or surrender of self-preference to the Creator's will, we chose self-sovereignty.

We decided we would do what we wanted to do, and that we would do it our way. With that choice came knowledge of good and evil and an awareness of disobeying God. Innocence gone; we freely rejected God. This choice created a change in the hearts of the first parents and in the hearts of all of their future children.

Now, instead of initially preferring God's will and plan, we preferred our own.

The Results

With our choice came moral knowledge of right and wrong. We awakened to our disobedience. What a heavy burden; what a consequence. Divine fellowship ended. No more long walks in the garden with Him. Innocence vanished in the shadow of selfish choice; with innocence went holiness. We broke loose from God and died spiritually—exactly what God said would happen. God had not lied to Eve after all. For as Oswald Chambers put it, "Sin is blatant mutiny against God."[2]

Deprived of God's presence, our hearts became depraved deep within. We found ways to live without God's immediate presence. We went our own way and did our own thing. The construction of the Tower of Babel proves that. We broke God's laws and broke God's heart whenever His ways for us conflicted with what we wanted to do.

Adam and Eve soon realized something in their hearts moved them to act differently. This difference was also manifested in their children. Instead of seeking God's will, their older son chose to do things his own way. Cain murdered his brother, Abel, out of selfish desires.

From Adam and Eve's day until today, very little has changed in the human heart. We are still born with a bent toward self-preference. We are still deprived of God's immediate presence. We still have depraved hearts. We are spiritually needy.

If you don't believe it, leaf through today's newspaper. Read story after story of parents abusing children, of children killing children, of lying and stealing, of street drugs and gang crimes. It's a heartbreaking, sad picture. Unfortunately, it's a worldwide problem. Michel de Montaigne accurately said, "Every man carries the entire form of the human condition."[3]

Some people tell me they do not believe sin is a universal problem—pervasive maybe, but not universal. I ask them if it's not universal then why can't the tabloid reporters or television news crews find us one example of a good person who never sinned against God and His plan. They cannot find even one example because the sin problem *is* universal. Only Jesus successfully avoided it.

The Experiment

I don't care who you are. I don't care how big you are. You are not going to tell me what I can and cannot do.

I'll never forget one day when our son Brent was a toddler. Sue placed a flower arrangement in the middle of the living room coffee table. Brent contentedly played in the floor with several toys near the coffee table. Then, he spotted the flower arrangement and immediately reasoned that it was more interesting than his toys.

I thought it would be educational to test his willpower with a fatherly admonition. I said, "Brent, do not touch the flowers." He looked at me, then at the flowers, then back at me. With the sternest look in my eye I could muster, I said,

"No" and shook my head to reinforce the importance of my admonition. He immediately quit exploring the flower arrangement and went back to playing with his toys. He apparently understood the message, or so I thought.

I then moved to the dining room and watched him from an inconspicuous location. The minute I left the room, he lunged for the coffee table and dove into that flower arrangement with both hands. He grabbed it as if he were embracing a big teddy bear.

I stepped into the living room and calmly asked, "What are you doing?"

As long as I live, I will never forget that look in his eye as our eyes met. His body language shouted to me in no uncertain terms, "I don't care who you are. I don't care how big you are. You are not going to tell me what I can and cannot do."

As much as I hated to admit it, I had to come to terms that day with the fact that my precious little boy, the pride and joy of my life, had "The Infection" from Adam and Eve.

What Is It?

What is this infection? How do we get it? How many of us get it? Where did it come from? The infection twists our thinking to prefer what we want more than what anyone else, including God, wants for us. It drives from the very core of our being to hold the control stick of our lives. It says to God the same message Brent's look said to me: "I don't care who you are. I don't care how big you are. You are not going to tell me what I can and cannot do."

Every one of us gets this infection just by being born into the world. It's the universal human problem of sin. It's a very part of our nature from the garden days. Like rebellious teenagers, we rebelled against our Creator Parent.

Why do we keep going on like this? I remember a time during Brent's teen years when I scolded him for doing something wrong. I said, "Son, why did you do that?" With a look of mystery in his eye that chilled me to the bone, he said, "I don't know, Dad. I don't know why I did it." And neither do any of the rest of us.

Anytime we defy God's will and break God's heart, we affirm our preference for self-sovereignty. It's so natural. So we keep doing it without knowing or caring why. All the self-help books in the bookstore, all of the personal counseling of the best counselors, all of the sternest resolutions to do better fail to break the cycle.

Bad News—Good News

So, what can we do to help ourselves? Not much. We can exercise large quantities of willpower, or we can turn over a tree full of new leaves. But that's about it. Only God's power can radically change the core of our beings with His forgiveness and grace.

> *It's a bad news/good news message.*

But, are we hopelessly programmed from the garden to repeat our mistakes over and over? Is forgiveness the best God can do for us? Must we always prefer our ways over God's ways? Is it a hopeless battle? A thousand times, No!

Here's the really good news of this book. Here's where the message of holiness comes in. Not only can God forgive us of our past sins, but He can also change us from within and reorient our nature so we can return to His will and plan for our lives. He heals us of "The Infection." He restores us to the way He originally intended us to be in the garden. No, we don't have physical walks with God every day, but we do fellowship continually with Him through His Holy Spirit. Now we are no longer deprived of His presence. Now we are forgiven of breaking God's law and His heart. Now our hearts can be cleansed from self-preference. Now we can be what God wants us to be—not by ourselves, but by the strength and power of His Holy Spirit living within us.

It's a bad news/good news message. The bad news is, "We're infected." The good news is, "God can heal us."

Supersaints?

We began this chapter by talking about God's plan for our holiness to follow a pattern like His holiness. What about that?

When we talk about realizing God's plan for our holiness, are we talking about possessing something that makes us holier than our friends? Does it make us supersaints? Does something change us into some sort of little holy god?

Not at all! We never possess a quality or an attribute that we own that characterizes us as holy. Ours is always a reflected holiness, much like moonlight. The moon has no light source at its core. It shines with light only as it remains connected to the sun. No sunlight—no moonlight.

We can be holy only as long as we live in relationship with the Father and let the light of His holiness shine through us. It's ours only as a gift from Him. That's why relationship with God is so important. If we have any hope of being holy, this is possible only as we live close to Him. When we live that way, we begin to look and act more like Him. As the old saying goes, "Like Father, like children."

Becoming like the God We Serve

I learned a very important lesson in a freshman college literature class while reading the *Odyssey* by Homer. Homer told of the adventures of Odysseus, who was lost at sea and wandering away from home for 20 years. Odysseus wandered from one adventure to another, each a little more dramatic than the previous. In each adventure, he encountered a different mythical god. He dealt with Zeus, Athena, Cyclops, Poseidon, and others.

> *We become like the god we serve.*

The gods responded to Odysseus differently. Sometimes they listened to his cries; sometimes they didn't. Sometimes they answered his prayers; sometimes they mocked him. Sometimes they responded with love; sometimes with hate. Sometimes they were kind and benevolent; sometimes they were spiteful, capricious, and vengeful. Odysseus never quite knew what to expect from the gods and goddesses of each adventure.

Here's the spiritual lesson I learned as I read those ancient stories. The ancient heroes of Greek and Roman mythology became like the gods they served. The gods led their followers into actions that were sometimes good and at other times bad. The mortals took on the character of the god who directed those actions.

I've studied the idea through the years and found it true across the board, in every land and with every religion. We become like the god we serve. That's why the concept of holiness is so important for Christians. We will never understand many things about God this side of eternity. However, the Bible makes one thing perfectly clear—our God is a holy God. He said, "Be holy because I, the LORD your God, am holy" (Lev. 19:2).

What better thing could happen to us than to become like the God we serve? That's another reason to properly understand holiness. It helps us reconnect with God's original plan for us.

Fast Takes

1. God has our best interest in mind. He wants us to find untarnished fulfillment in daily living.

2. Without Him at the center, life never makes sense.

3. With free will we can choose to love and obey God or to break His heart.

4. Given the option of self-sovereignty or surrender of self-preference to the Creator's will, we choose self-sovereignty.

5. "The Infection" twists or bends our thinking to prefer what we want more than what God wants.

6. The bad news is "We're infected." The good news is "God can heal us."

7. We become like the God we serve.

Think About This . . .

1. Give examples of the effects of "The Infection" you have seen in your own life or the lives of your friends and loved ones.

2. Plato, the Greek philosopher, taught: "To know right is to do it." Do you agree or disagree with this philosophy? Give examples.

3. How is this philosophy taught and believed today?

4. What would lead you to believe "The Infection" is a universal problem of all humanity?

5. Analyze the serpent's strategy. What was it? Why was it so successful?

6. Why do you think Adam and Eve chose to eat the forbidden fruit?

7. In what ways was the serpent's appeal to Adam and Eve similar to the way Satan tempts us today?

8. Why does this appeal continue to work after thousands of years?

9. Why do we keep falling for the appeal over and over again?

10. Why do people choose their will over God's will? What is the attraction?

Holy, holy, holy is the LORD Almighty;
the whole earth is full of his glory.
—*Seraphs speaking to Isaiah*
(Isa. 6:3)

3

WHO IS HE?

The Game Show

I remember when I was a kid, I watched an old black-and-white game show on television. The program host started the show by telling a name and a profession. He then introduced three contestants, who all claimed to be the person with that profession. Four celebrities asked the three contestants questions to figure out which contestant truly owned that name and profession. The studio audience and viewers at home tried to beat the celebrities at the game.

That's a bit like the way the Bible introduces God to us. It describes God with many colorful words and shows Him in action in various peoples' lives and in world events. It talks about God's likes and dislikes, along with His desires for His creation. Then, with this information in place, the Bible invites us to find this God in our world and in our personal lives. It urges us to discover personal relationship with Him.

Before we get too far with our amazing adventure story, we need to look more closely at God. We should explore more about how He wants to relate to us along with the plans He has for us. Since God and holiness appear so closely together in the Bible, we also need to take time to see how God defines and energizes the concept of holiness. With that understanding in place, we can better continue our adventure story.

The Defining Attribute

Who is this holy God, our Creator, with whom we are getting reacquainted? We really ought to learn all we can about Him since we are created in His image. As we learn more about Him, we learn more about His plans for us.

Many books have been written about God's nature and character. In fact, no amount of human effort could ever produce all that should be said to properly understand God. So, we will limit our discussion about

God to holiness. Holiness is not simply one positive God-quality among many; it defines all of God's other attributes or characteristics. Holiness defines God the way light defines the sun. It is the essence of who He is. From His holiness flow all of God's other attributes, such as truth, love, mercy, grace, and righteousness.

Let me illustrate. The psalmist said, "And the heavens proclaim his righteousness" (Ps. 50:6). When we say God is righteous, we mean He follows the moral rules He has established. He always does the right thing. So God's holiness guarantees righteous actions.

God's grace and mercy flow from His holiness in that He shows compassion on us in our unholy spiritual condition, and He acts kindly toward us when we deserve judgment. His holiness gives us what we do not deserve (grace) and does not give us what we do deserve (mercy). Paul reminded us, "For it is by grace you have been saved, through faith—and this not from yourselves, it is the gift of God" (Eph. 2:8).

As we discussed in chapter 1, the concept of holiness usually scares people. It drives distance between itself and unholiness, the way light drives away darkness. A great chasm separates holiness from everything inferior. But God's love closes the abyss between His holiness and our unholiness and draws us to His loving heart. The fact that "God is love" (1 John 4:16) reminds us that He reached out to us before we even knew we needed Him, and He held out hope to change our unholiness into holiness. His holy love wishes to share himself with His loved ones. So, He offers us this holy gift.

God's love closes the abyss between His holiness and our unholiness and draws us to His loving heart.

God is truth (John 14:6). Truth flows from God's holiness, so we can rely on what He says to be correct. He never lies, misrepresents, or misleads us. He never says, "Cross my heart; I'm telling the truth this time." He always tells the truth. He works with all of the facts and always judges them accurately to reach correct conclusions. So when His Word tells us that God loves us or is gracious and merciful to us, we know these statements are factual. Because God is holy, He always bears truth.

We could demonstrate the concept a hundred other ways, but you get the picture. Holiness threads its way through all of God's other attributes to help define them.

God's Holiness in the Bible

Genesis does not speak specifically about God's holiness, but hints at it in various ways. For example, when Adam and Eve sinned against God, they hid from Him in fear (Gen. 3:8-10). Unholiness always hides from holiness. Noah is referred to as a righteous and blameless man who walked with God (6:9). Noah pleased God because he was righteous and blameless. God called Abram to be blameless, a quality God desires in humanity (17:1). Jacob encountered God's presence at Bethel as he ran from his angry brother Esau. This presence filled him with fear as he found himself on holy ground (28:16-17). He felt unworthy in the presence of holiness.

We begin to hear specifically about holiness in Exodus when Moses stood before the burning bush. As the Lord talked to Moses through this miraculous bush that flamed without being consumed, He told Moses, "Take off your sandals, for the place where you are standing is holy ground" (Exod. 3:5). God's presence made the ground holy. After the miraculous crossing of the Red Sea, Moses sang, "Who among the gods is like you, O LORD? Who is like you—majestic in holiness, awesome in glory, working wonders?" (15:11).

> **God's presence made the ground holy.**

Our understanding of God's holiness takes further shape as we read Leviticus. Many things about this book mystify us. It speaks of symbols and images that make no sense to our modern minds. Reading Leviticus can sometimes seem like trying to read a foreign language. Yet, the holiness of God, and His hopes and dreams for our holiness, set the backdrop of the entire book. All of the unusual symbols and images point toward holiness in one way or another.

For example we read, "I am the LORD your God; consecrate yourselves and be holy, because I am holy. Do not make yourselves unclean by any creature that moves about on the ground. I am the LORD who brought you up out of Egypt to be your God; therefore be holy, because I am holy" (Lev. 11:44-45). Or again God says, "You are to be holy to me because I, the LORD, am holy, and I have set you apart from the nations to be my own" (20:26). "Consider them holy, because I the LORD am holy—I who make you holy" (21:8).

These last two verses contribute to what is called the Holiness Code in Leviticus. This code constantly reminds the Hebrew people that wherever they go and whatever they do, they must never forget one thing— God is holy. It might interest you to know that other verses in the Leviticus Holiness Code include 21:15; 21:23; 22:9; 22:16; and 22:32. Our call to holiness in Leviticus stems from God's holiness.

The Psalms frequently reference the holiness of God. Everything related to God becomes holy, such as His holy hill (Ps. 3:4), His holy Temple (5:7; 11:4), His holy heaven (20:6), His holy place (28:2), and His holy mountain (43:3). But, more importantly, Psalms links God's holiness and His name. For example, "Sing to the LORD, you saints of his; praise his holy name" (30:4). "Let them praise your great and awesome name—he is holy. . . . Exalt the LORD our God and worship at his footstool; he is holy. . . . Exalt the LORD our God and worship at his holy mountain, for the LORD our God is holy" (99:3, 5, 9).

A Complete Picture

One of the most complete pictures of God's holiness occurred in the life of the prophet Isaiah. The story comes from Isa. 6:1-8:

In the year that King Uzziah died, I saw the Lord seated on a throne, high and exalted, and the train of his robe filled the temple. Above him were seraphs, each with six wings: With two wings they covered their faces, with two they covered their feet, and with two they were flying. And they were calling to one another: "Holy, holy, holy is the LORD Almighty; the whole earth is full of his glory." At the sound of their voices the doorposts and thresholds shook and the temple was filled with smoke.

"Woe to me!" I cried. "I am ruined! For I am a man of unclean lips, and I live among a people of unclean lips, and my eyes have seen the King, the LORD Almighty."

Then one of the seraphs flew to me with a live coal in his hand, which he had taken with tongs from the altar. With it he touched my mouth and said, "See, this has touched your lips; your guilt is taken away and your sin atoned for."

Then I heard the voice of the Lord saying, "Whom shall I send? And who will go for us?"

And I said, "Here am I. Send me!"

Isaiah was no stranger to religious life; he served in the ministry. But on this particular day he caught a glimpse of God's holiness unlike anything he'd ever seen. He'd attended many meaningful worship services in which he sensed God's presence, but nothing like this! Isaiah's mind was blown as he saw the holy radiance of this awesome One. When he saw how holy and spotless God appeared, he couldn't help but look at himself. He did not like what he saw; he didn't measure up. He needed something in his life that his religion had not given him to this point.

Once he caught this glimpse of Holy God, he could never be satisfied with remaining the same.

Isaiah's experience gives us a pretty clear image of our holy God. Let's also notice with Isaiah that we can't come into God's holy presence and remain the same. Isaiah's divine encounter transformed him. What an example for us! Even a glimpse of God raises the bar on where we should be.

Whether it's the "holy, holy, holy" of Isa. 6:3 in the Old Testament or of Rev. 4:8 in the New Testament, the idea is the same. God is holy at the very core of His being.

The Meanings of God's Holiness

How does the Bible picture God's holiness? As we analyze the biblical terms used in reference to God's holiness, we discover three main ideas.

1. *God is high and lifted up.* The Bible often describes God as sitting on a majestic throne. People in the Old Testament attributed great power and authority to the king's throne. The throne sat in a prominent place in a castle room designated only for it (1 Kings 7:7). The throne sat on a raised platform with several steps leading up to it (2 Chron. 9:18). Precious commodities such as ivory and gold covered it (v. 17).

God has just such a throne in heaven. From this lofty and sacred position our holy God watches over all creation. Hear the psalmist as he describes, "God reigns over the nations; God is seated on his holy throne" (Ps. 47:8) and "Righteousness and justice are the foundation of your throne; love and faithfulness go before you" (89:14).

These twin foundations of God's throne remind us that He always does what is right, and He judges those who do wrong. Both concepts of doing right and judgment for wrongdoing fold into a biblical concept of God's holiness.

2. *God shines as a bright light.* He imaged himself to Moses as a bright fire in the burning bush (Exod. 3:2). At the giving of the Ten Commandments, God descended on Mount Sinai and appeared to the children of Israel as a bright fire (19:18). Moses spent extended periods of time with the Lord on Mount Sinai when he received the Ten Commandments. He asked God if he could see His glory. God indicated that His glory was too bright for human eyes. So, God compromised and let Moses see His backside as He passed by (33:18-23). Moses' encounter with God's glory, though brief, made his own face shine with a bright glow. He had to wear a veil over his face when he talked to the Israelites (34:29-35).

Following their departure from Egypt, God lived with His children in the Tabernacle and filled it with His glory through the wilderness wandering. This glory appeared as a cloud consuming the Tabernacle. Moses and the people could not enter the holy place because the presence of the Lord so strongly filled it (40:34-35).

3. *God is pure.* He does not defile himself with sin or anything that would dilute His character. Habakkuk declared, "Your eyes are too pure to look on evil; you cannot tolerate wrong" (1:13).

God calls us to this same purity. "Surely God is good to Israel, to those who are pure in heart" (Ps. 73:1). Jesus reminded us, "Blessed are the pure in heart, for they will see God" (Matt. 5:8). John also called for this quality of God to be imitated in us. "Everyone who has this hope in him purifies himself, just as he is pure" (1 John 3:3).

Set Apart for God

This holy God reserves things for himself. He sets things apart for His use or enjoyment. They remain separate from the secular or profane. They are not the run-of-the-mill discount store closeout items. They are special because they belong to God. Because of this unique place they occupy in His sight, these things are referred to in the Bible as holy or sacred. A partial list of these holy things includes: the high priest's garments (Exod. 28:2), the Tabernacle and all the objects in it (40:9), the tithe (Lev. 27:32), the Sabbath (Exod. 35:3; Isa. 58:13), the place of the ark of the testimony (Exod. 26:33), Jerusalem (Isa. 48:2), the Temple (Matt. 24:15), and Scripture (Rom. 1:2).

They are not the run-of-the-mill discount store closeout items. They are special because they belong to God.

The high priest treated as sacred the garments he wore while conducting worship of God. Ezekiel gave an example of this. The high priest wore special clothing during the worship service. When the service ended, he changed his clothes and left the sacred garments in the holy place of worship. Even the priest's clothing that contacted holy God were too special for street wear (Ezek. 44:19).

The Tabernacle and Temple altars draw particular interest because of their holy nature. Not only are these altars of the Lord considered holy, but also any objects placed on them as offerings to God become holy by their very contact with the altars. Moses spoke for God to the children of Israel, "For seven days make atonement for the altar and consecrate it. Then the altar will be most holy, and whatever touches it will be holy" (Exod. 29:37).

Jesus reemphasized this concept when He said, "Which is greater: the gold, or the temple that makes the gold sacred? . . . Which is greater: the gift, or the altar that makes the gift sacred?" (Matt. 23:17, 19).

This whole notion of something being holy because it is set apart for God is often referred to as the priestly concept of holiness. This is because the priests themselves personified the Tabernacle or Temple, and all of the objects in the Tabernacle and Temple were associated with worship of God. Everything set apart for God received reverence.

> *We would never think of taking the church's offering plates and serving dog food in them to the pastor's puppy.*

We carry this notion into modern time. We set the offering plates at the local church apart for collecting tithes and offerings for God. We would never think of taking the church's offering plates and using them to serve dog food to the pastor's puppy. My dad and mom never let me or my friends chase each other in the church sanctuary. They taught us reverence for the Lord's house.

This priestly concept of holiness directly applies to our lives. The Old Testament Tabernacle and Temple, along with all of the objects associated with worship of God, belonged to Him and thus were set apart for His holy purposes. So we see in this God's desire to share His holiness with His creation.

We, too, can belong to Him and can be set apart for Him. We, too, can become holy. Being set apart for God is a biblical concept that originates in God's holiness.

Big and Scary

My friend Barbara used to have the biggest, meanest-looking dog you ever saw. He looked like a small pony. Max was a black Doberman pinscher with a mouthful of shark's teeth. His sight alone struck fear into the hearts of men and boys alike. Barbara kept him around the house not only for company but also for protection.

Max made a great companion but was a worthless guard dog. He only looked mean. He didn't have a mean bone in his oversized body. He was just an overgrown puppy who loved to play in the backyard and have you scratch under his neck. Many people probably kept their distance from Barbara and Max simply because of preconceived notions about big, black dogs. They couldn't have been more wrong about Max.

People also have preconceived notions about God and His holiness. Those notions keep them running from God the way folks ran from Max.

True, from the beginning of the Bible to the end, we find frequent testimony to God's holiness. You can't learn anything about God and avoid His holiness. You can't come in contact with Him and miss it. His holiness flows from the core of His being and affects the way He responds to His creation.

However, we must always remember holiness is not intended to separate us from Him. Holiness hopes to separate us from sin and join us to God. That was His plan from the very beginning—to fellowship intimately with us every day. So, His holy love draws us to His holy heart. His holy grace and mercy forgive us of our many sins so we can stand acceptable in His sight. The fact that God is holy should not scare us away from Him the way it scared Adam and Eve in the garden. It should draw us to His side just as our loving Heavenly Father planned all long.

Fast Takes

1. Holiness defines all of God's attributes and characteristics.
2. References to God's holiness fill the Bible.
3. God's holiness means He is high and lifted up, shines as a bright light, and is pure.
4. God never intends His holiness to separate us from Him; He hopes to separate us from sin and join us to Him.

Think About This . . .

1. Find ways to compare our holiness to being a reflection of God's holiness.
2. Why is relationship with God so important to our holiness?
3. Complete this sentence: When I think about how holy God is, I feel . . .
4. Complete this sentence: When I hear that I'm supposed to be holy like God is, I feel . . .
5. Is God's call for us to be holy realistic?
6. Is God's call for us to be holy possible?
7. Would God call us to something that is neither realistic nor possible?

The Lord doesn't want
the first place in my life,
He wants all of my life.
—*Howard Amerding*[1]

4

THE CURE

He Couldn't Seem to Help himself

I learned a hard lesson about addictive behavior when I was a small boy. I grew up on a farm, and like most farm boys I had a pet dog. He was just a black and white mutt, but Button was my best friend. We played together every day after school and all summer long. I loved that dog!

One day my dad sat me down at the kitchen table and told me he had to kill by best friend. It seems my little buddy had gone into the neighbor's henhouse and helped himself to a nest full of freshly laid eggs. I thought the death penalty was a little severe for a few lost eggs. Then, my dad said something I have never forgotten. "Once a dog gets a taste of fresh eggs, you'll never keep him out of the hen house. He's hooked for life."

I begged my dad to try something else before killing Button. So, dad agreed to spare his life by moving him 30 miles from our farmhouse. But a few days later Button strolled right back up to our front door with a big grin on his face and tail wagging as if to say, "I'm back!"

Then dad took him even further in another direction. Again, he returned like a boomerang. Thinking his world travels might have helped his addictive egg-sucking behavior, I talked my dad into a probation period for Button. The next week, Button was right back in the neighbor's henhouse. He couldn't seem to help himself—he'd tasted fresh eggs. Button met his maker that morning with wet eggs still on his nose.

Am I like That?

Am I in just as bad a condition as Button? Once I've tasted sin, am I hopelessly programmed to repeat my past mistakes over and over for as long as I live? Do I have to always prefer my ways over God's ways? Will I always use my free will to choose my own way?

Some Christians believe sin's addictive power is greater than God's healing power. They think that once we touch sin to our lips, we're doomed to repeat our past mistakes as long as we live. Sin throws us into a hopeless cycle and stains our hearts beyond repair in this life.

My mother used to say, "Lie down with dogs and you'll get up with fleas." Once we've laid with sin, these folks believe we must live with sins' fleas until life on earth ends. It's a very sad picture.

> *Lie down with dogs and you'll get up with fleas.*

In chapter 2 we talked about the bad news—we're infected with sin. We've tasted forbidden fruit.

But, we didn't stop there. We also talked about some very good news—God can heal us from this infection. He can forgive us of our past sins. All Christians believe that. So, you aren't likely to enter a heated discussion with your Christian friends on whether God forgives us or not when we ask Him.

But you might enter just such a disagreeable discussion when you mention the next point: More than just forgiveness, God can change us from within, at a heart level, to break the cycle of sin. In this way, we can please Him and live according to that original plan we've talked so much about—that plan from the garden days.

This powerful God-change appears to be the very idea the prophet Zechariah, father of John the Baptist, had in mind when he looked ahead to the ministry of Jesus. He said Jesus would come "To rescue us from the hand of our enemies, and to enable us to serve him without fear in holiness and righteousness before him all our days" (Luke 1:74-75). Notice that holiness and right living appear together as God's goals for us with Christ's coming. Holiness changes our heart; right living results in our daily conduct.

When does this happen? At the end of our earthly lives? When we get to heaven? No. This can happen in us right now. Not just the last few days or on good days, but *all* our days. That means right here on earth, right now. That's the power of the gospel of Jesus Christ working in us!

How does God do this?

God's Plan of Salvation

God's plan of salvation—to restore us to the original intention He had for us—begins with faith in Jesus Christ. As we trust in Christ's death on Calvary and His resurrection from the dead, the Father forgives us of our past sins and adopts us into His family. As we walk in daily fellowship with Him, we are no longer deprived of His presence, which Adam and Eve lost in the garden exit.

Like the television advertisers say, "But wait. There's more." Forgiveness is wonderful, but it is not enough. Like Grandpa used to say, "You can't get the worm out of the apple by polishing the apple." We need to be more than polished; we need the worm out. That is, we need God's power to break sin's hold over us and reorient us from within, so we can continue to live every day like His child. When? Not some days, not on good days alone, but "all our days."

Sin creates a twofold problem. God's forgiveness takes care of my past acts of sinning. That long list constitutes problem number one. But what about sin's nature buried deep within me that causes me to want to do the wrong thing or "my thing" in the first place? What about that pride that boasts to the world, "I did it my way!" That's problem number two. Preference for self-sovereignty lurks at the heart of this matter.

> *I just want to retain some autonomy about life's direction.*

That self-preference remains deeply rooted in my nature even after God forgives the list of sins. I enjoy God's forgiveness and fellowship, but part of me wants to retain at least some control of my life. After all, it is my life isn't it?

This attitude or mind-set highlights this second problem that needs God's touch. It's not that I want to go out in the dark of the night and sin against Him. It's not that I wish to rebel against Him. I'm not hoping to harbor some sinful habit or spirit. I just want to retain some autonomy about life's direction. Why should someone else get to call the shots in my life? Why should I have to surrender control of everything?

Complete Control

Early in my marriage to Sue, I learned an important lesson about a fundamental difference between us. She likes things in our house to be organized: clothes folded neatly in her dresser drawers; items stacked in her closet; dishes organized in her kitchen.

Unfortunately, I didn't inherit the "organized and in order" gene. No problem as long as I was unmarried. It didn't play out very well once we married and started living under the same roof, however. Her orderliness seemed a little excessive to me; my disorderliness seemed like the actions of a slob to her. So, we reached a compromise in those early days of marriage that works to this very day.

Here's what we decided. The floor space of our house that she manages is to be kept organized; the floor space that I manage can be any way I want it to be. She manages the kitchen, living room, bedrooms, and other rooms of the house. I manage the garage, toolshed, and my dresser drawers (the places nobody sees!). Granted, my areas are not large, compared to the rest of the house, but they're mine—all mine to do with as I please. We never disagree about my areas because I have control over them. We keep her areas clean; she stays fairly clear of my not-so-clean areas.

What does that illustration have to do with holiness? Everything. You see, when we give our hearts and lives to Christ in conversion, we give Him everything of ourselves that we know to give Him at the time. We're so anxious to be free from the guilt and bondage of sin that we're willing to sign just about any contract He sets before us, much like we're willing to sign loan papers when bills pile up and the money's all gone.

Then, we begin to clean up all of life's areas (actions, thoughts, attitudes, motives, reactions, possessions, habits, and all the rest). They all fall under Christ's oversight. Unfortunately, we usually move a few personal items to one very small room in our lives. Not anything big and bad, just a prideful attitude, a sour spirit, or an unhealthy habit. The items don't matter. The issue is that they represent our autonomy.

Wouldn't you know it! When we start getting really serious with God and deeply involved in Christian living, He asks for the key to that little room we call our own. We've willingly given Him the keys to every other room in the house of our lives, but that's not enough for Him. He wants all of the keys, not just 99 percent of them.

Oh yes, I forgot to tell you one important point about my little compromise with Sue. She doesn't have a key to the toolshed, so she can't get in there and organize my yard tools. That wouldn't be a bad idea except that I want the tools organized *my way*. We cannot be totally sold out to God and keep even one key. In time, He'll put His finger on that one key and ask for it too.

George D. Watson once said this sellout consists of three commitments: "To be anything the Lord wants us to be, to do anything the Lord wants us to do, and to suffer anything the Lord wants us to suffer."[2] That's a mouthful!

I probably will not know I have a "key" problem in my spiritual life for a long time. Such a problem may reside undetected within me for months or even years of travel down life's road with Christ. But, if I continue to read my Bible, pray, attend church regularly, and enjoy the spiritual blessings of God, the key problem will eventually surface to my immediate attention. When I recognize this attitude or mind-set as a hindrance in my spiritual progress and realize I need to resolve it, I place myself in an excellent position for God to help me.

Again, the solution to sin problem number two is to surrender the
control center of my life. I must let God have complete control of my entire life: past, present, and future, everything I am
and everything I may ever become. I must surrender all my hopes, dreams, goals, and aspirations to
His leadership. He gets all of the keys. It's what the
old-timers called surrendering "the unknown bun-
dle" to God. It's the thrust of the quote by Howard
Amerding at the beginning of this chapter.

> **He gets all the keys!**

But How Does God Work This Miracle?

How does God work a miracle of grace on "The Infection" with
which sin grips me? That's somewhat of a spiritual mystery. God first requires the expectation of our faith. Just as I trusted Christ to forgive my
past sins, so I trust Him to accept when I offer myself more fully to Him.
The following passages of Scripture enlighten this thought:

> Therefore, I urge you, brothers, in view of God's mercy, to offer
> your bodies as living sacrifices, holy and pleasing to God—this is
> your spiritual act of worship *(Rom. 12:1).*

> May God himself, the God of peace, sanctify you through and
> through. May your whole spirit, soul and body be kept blameless at
> the coming of our Lord Jesus Christ. The one who calls you is faithful
> and he will do it *(1 Thess. 5:23-24).*

The first passage speaks of our offer; the second of God's sanctifying
work. We call our offer *consecration.* This is when we present ourselves
to God in a new and sacrificial way. Just as objects were laid on the altars
of the Tabernacle and Temple to be given to God, so we lay ourselves fig-
uratively on God's altar to offer ourselves to Him for whatever He might
wish to do with us. Consecration, then, involves our act of making ourselves available to God as a component of our worship of Him.

The second biblical passage speaks of God sanctifying us. *Sanctification* and related words, such as *sanctify, holy,* and *holiness,* occur in the
Bible more than 1,100 times. Scripture often repeats the concept. In both
biblical languages of Old Testament Hebrew and New Testament Greek,
words such as *holiness* and *sanctification* are used somewhat inter-
changeably. They do, however, convey different meanings in English.

Holiness comes from an old English word also translated "whole,"
"health," or "hallow." So, it refers to being whole, in good health, or
holy. Basically, *sanctification* refers to the total, lifelong process of becoming holy. It's all God does in us to restore our hearts to the way He
created us to be. The point at which God sanctifies us wholly refers to a

particular point in time when we consecrate ourselves fully to God and give up the stronghold of self-preference. So *holiness* is a broad term, *sanctification* more focused.

My spiritual self-seeking, self-willed, self-sufficient ways have to go. They are replaced by a new availability to all God wants for me. Thus, holiness is the condition of our soul and characterization of our lifestyle, which results from God's work of sanctification.

Offering ourselves to God sounds like a simple act. But is it really? What if God asked me to give a lot of time and money to the church? What if He asked me to serve Him in a third-world country without air conditioning, ice, and with really big bugs? What if I gave Him total control of everything, and He turned my world upside down?

Well, if I'm really serious about consecrating myself fully to Him, that's OK. Whatever He asks, I'm willing. I'm just a glove for His hand to fill. Remember, He gets all of the keys.

The Symbol and Its Reality

The discussion of altars and sacrifices brings to mind the entire Old Testament sacrificial system. The system was designed to bring people to God and make them right in His sight. So, year by year, animal sacrifices were brought to the altars of the Tabernacle and the Temple by the thousands. The animals died, the blood spilled, and the meat was offered to the flames. However, the people went home year after year without feeling any different inside, not knowing whether their sins were actually forgiven. The ritual did not seem to change anything down deep inside their souls.

Christ's sacrifice of himself was the best sacrifice of all!

You see, the sacrificial system did well at defining the sin problem. It made people feel guilty when they measured their lives against the law. It pointed to their deep spiritual need and hunger. But, it couldn't get down deep enough to solve the problem, actually forgive the sins, and bring inner freedom. It only pointed worshipers in the right direction, set them on a journey, then left them stranded along the roadside.

This is the problem addressed by the writer to the Hebrews in 10:1-4. He says the law was a shadow, not the reality. It pointed to something beyond itself. That's why all the sacrifices year after year didn't actually forgive sins and cleanse away guilt; they couldn't go that far. Scripture finally concludes, "It is impossible for the blood of bulls and goats to take away sins" (v. 4).

We know today that's true, but worshipers in the Old Testament didn't know any better. They only knew the sacrificial system. So they hoped that one more animal sacrifice this year would remove the guilt and bring inner freedom. It didn't. That's why they kept returning. They found themselves caught up in a hopeless cycle. How sad!

Thankfully, when Christ came, He changed all that. His sacrifice of himself became the best sacrifice of all, the most complete in every way. The perfect Son of God completed the entire Old Testament sacrificial system with His own sacrifice. He replaced the symbol with the reality, like taking a picture of a new red sports car to the downtown automobile showroom and trading it for the real thing.

Thus the writer of Hebrews says, "He sets aside the first to establish the second" (10:9). Something wonderful happens in us as a result of this perfect sacrifice, something the Old Testament system could never even dream of accomplishing. That is, "We have been made holy through the sacrifice of the body of Jesus Christ once for all" (v. 10).

This, then, focuses our understanding for the secret of how God makes us holy. Our holiness has its root in Jesus Christ's obedience to the Father's salvation plan. According to that plan Jesus offered himself as a sacrifice for the world's sins. He obeyed the Father. We identify with Christ and sacrifice ourselves to God just as He did. God accepts our efforts not as efforts on our own strength, but as faith steps of following our perfect example, Jesus, and letting Him direct us.

Jesus Christ, the Holy One, lives in and through us and, in so doing, makes us holy. His life in us. Wow! Again, we see this as His holiness reflected through us the way the moon reflects the light of the sun.

> **This is the message of full salvation from sin.**

Although the Old Testament priests continued to make sacrifices day after day, year after year, they could not dig to the bottom of the sin problem (vv. 11-12). Jesus, on the other hand, made His sacrifice once and sat down at the right hand of God. "Because by one sacrifice he has made perfect forever those who are being made holy" (v. 14).

Here again we find the message of full salvation from sin. Here again we see God's plan to bring us back to himself. We don't have to wait for the death angel's knock to receive this blessed hope. Through Christ's sacrifice on the Cross we can find our sins forgiven, be identified with the perfect sacrifice, and receive holiness of heart. This is not something we do ourselves by keeping a list of laws. Folks in the Old Testament tried that and failed. It's something we receive as a gift from God, simply for the trusting. We accept God's gift and live in the fullness of it.

Maybe it's just human nature. But, we're often tempted to think we can earn or deserve our salvation in some small way. Sure, we're willing to accept initial forgiveness as a gift, but we want to earn our keep the rest of the way. We try to earn our salvation by diligently serving in the church, sacrificially giving time and money to the work of the Kingdom, or making extra efforts in some ministry endeavor.

This scripture passage in Hebrews reminds us that we don't earn or deserve any part of our salvation. It's all a God gift. Christ made the sacrifice; He paid the price. We simply accept it and live thankful lives.

So, that's the secret to full salvation from sin—both forgiveness for acts of sinning (sin problem number 1) and the inclination to sin in the first place (sin problem number 2). It's all made possible by Christ's sacrifice. He is the heart and soul of our holiness. And that's why I'm not like Button, my dog. Yes, I've enjoyed the sweet taste of sin. Don't kid yourself—Satan offers a very sweet product. But that sweetness soon turns to bitter, destructive poison; it always does. As Abigail Van Buren said, "While forbidden fruit is said to taste sweeter, it usually spoils faster."[3]

For some strange reason I kept going back to sin, even though I knew it was destroying me. I was no better than my drug addict friend who knew his habit threatened his life, but he kept taking the poison anyway.

Why? Who knows? I can't say; I did the same thing! I thought I was hopelessly programmed to repeat my mistakes for as long as I lived. I thought sin's addictive power was greater than God's healing power.

The good news of the gospel, "Therefore, there is now no condemnation for those who are in Christ Jesus, because through Christ Jesus the law of the Spirit of life set me free from the law of sin and death" (Rom. 8:1-2). God can heal us from "The Infection." He has the cure! John Wesley once said, "Know your disease; know your cure."[4] Thank God, we know both!

Fast Takes

1. Some Christians believe sin's addictive power is greater than God's healing power.

2. God can change us from within to break the cycle of sinning.

3. Sin's problem is twofold: acts of sinning and a preference for self-sovereignty, which is a manifestation of the sin nature.

4. In consecration we present ourselves to God in a new, sacrificial way.

5. Holiness is the condition of our soul and characterization of our lifestyle that results from God's work of sanctification.

6. The perfect Son of God completed the entire Old Testament sacrificial system with His own sacrifice.

7. Our holiness has its roots in the obedience of Jesus Christ to the Father's salvation plan.

8. Christ made the sacrifice; He paid the price. We simply accept it and live thankful lives.

Think About This . . .

1. How was Button's addictive behavior like the addictive behavior in people?

2. Give examples of friends or loved ones who seem helpless in the face of addictive behavior, even when they know it is destroying them.

3. Why is the idea so popular, even among many Christians, that people are powerless against temptation?

4. Why do many people believe that we are powerless against temptation's suggestions?

5. Why is the forgiveness of God not enough to solve sin's problem?

6. Give ways in which self-sovereignty, self-seeking, self-will, or self-sufficiency can find their way in a Christian's heart and life?

7. Why is self-sovereignty a hindrance to spiritual growth?

8. Why is it so hard for most of us to surrender self-preference to God?

9. Why is total self-surrender to God not as easy as it may appear on the surface?

You can't have a good idea
until you have a good dream.

A LONG-AWAITED DREAM COMES TRUE

My Friend's Move

Sondra and I became good friends during my teen years. We often talked at school and exchanged stories about homelife. I loved to hear about her home because she came from a very poor background. She occasionally described features of her house. Over time I gathered a composite picture. Not a very impressive portrait.

The place Sondra called home was only an old wooden shack, about 20 feet square. It had a front porch and two small bedrooms. Sondra and her sister occupied one bedroom, her parents the other. Her brother Tom slept on the living room couch. The old wooden floor had holes big enough for snakes to crawl through occasionally. The old uninsulated lap-sided walls had holes in them. Tiny beams of sunlight filtered through like water through a strainer. Some of the walls were papered with newspaper. You could read about events from days gone by all over the walls. An old toilet sat in the backyard.

Sondra often told me about her father's dream of building his family a new home. She described how it would look. I listened to her descriptions but never believed her family would ever move into their dream home. Her dad told her those stories to pass the time in the old shack.

Sondra and I didn't talk for several months. Then one day she approached me in the parking lot at school and said, "We just moved into our new dream home. Would you like to see it?"

"Boy, would I," I thought. I couldn't wait to see this!

Sondra lived far out in the country. I almost needed a native guide to find her address. She met me at the driveway to her old shack. She gave me a quick tour of the old thing. It was just as I had pictured it: a real dump!

Then we got in my car and drove across a dirt path through the field behind the shack. To this day, I still can't believe what I saw. There in the middle of the field stood a big, red-bricked southern mansion. Four white columns set off the two-story front porch. It looked like something out of a southern romance movie. We toured the interior and enjoyed a delicious meal Sondra's mother fixed for us. I drove home that evening realizing that a father's big dreams can come true!

Jesus' Promise

It all happened so fast. It seemed to the disciples like such an abrupt ending. Before Jesus' ministry had hardly started, He stood on the Mount of Olives telling them good-bye. Their hearts sagged with sorrow. They could hardly form words to properly close their time together. How do you wrap up something like this? Then He filled their ears and hearts with a message of promise and hope. "Do not leave Jerusalem, but wait for the gift my Father promised, which you have heard me speak about. For John baptized with water, but in a few days you will be baptized with the Holy Spirit" (Acts 1:4-5). He promised a new source of power for their Christian lives (v. 8). Then, like a rocket ship moving skyward, Jesus lifted from the ground and soon disappeared from the disciples' sight. He returned to His Father; the disciples felt all alone.

> *He filled their ears and hearts with a message of promise and hope.*

Then, they obeyed Jesus. They all gathered back in the Upper Room where they had celebrated the Last Supper with Jesus 40 days earlier, and they prayed together. This proved to be quite a unifying experience for Jesus' disciples. They had experienced some pretty trying times over the past several weeks. Now with Jesus absent from the group, they needed a new catalyst to draw them back together. They prayed through each day and into the evening for more than a week. They didn't know how long they would be together like this or exactly what to expect. Jesus seemed to indicate that when His promise reached its fulfillment among them they would have no doubt. So, they waited for something dramatic to happen.

The Promise Fulfilled

What an understatement! *Dramatic* doesn't begin to describe what took place. On the 10th day of the disciples' prayer meeting, the heavens broke open and the promised Holy Spirit filled them to the depth of their being (2:1-4). Just as God gave marvelous signs when He instituted a new contract with Moses, He gave the disciples marvelous signs with their new contract.

When God gave Moses the Ten Commandments, the Hebrew nation

put on clean clothes, prepared their hearts, and waited. On the third day of their wait, a dark cloud covered Mount Sinai. Out of the cloud came bright lightning, loud thunder, and a very loud trumpet blast. Smoke billowed from the mountain as fire descended from heaven. The mountain shook as if being ripped apart by an earthquake (Exod. 19:14-19). All of these sights and sounds signaled God's presence and power.

The Holy Spirit came upon them in ways they could never doubt.

The sights and sounds of Pentecost also signaled God's presence and power. A great wind blew through their prayer meeting, symbolizing power. Flames of fire descended upon each prayer meeting participant. These flames symbolized purity of heart.

All the disciples began proclaiming the gospel message in languages that they had never learned. They hit the streets and told the thousands of Jerusalem visitors about Jesus Christ. This symbolized the need to take the new gospel message to the ends of the earth, to every language group. Keep in mind, these were the same people who hid from the religious and civil authorities behind locked doors just a few days before. Now they were out in public, telling everyone who would listen about Jesus Christ.

Jesus had certainly fulfilled His Mount of Olives promise beyond their wildest imaginations. The Holy Spirit came upon them in ways they could never doubt. They literally talked about that day for the rest of their lives. We know this because when a council meeting of the Christian Church convened 20 years later, Peter was still rehearsing what the Holy Spirit did in their hearts on the Day of Pentecost and in the hearts of Gentiles who were later filled with the Holy Spirit (Acts 15:1-21). By that time the Church had spread far beyond the boundaries of Jerusalem, Israel, and the Middle East. It had gained strength in established congregations all over the Roman Empire and continued unrestrained growth and expansion.

The Christian Church no longer consisted of Jews alone, as in the beginning. Countless Gentiles also called themselves Christians. Peter, in speaking to the Jerusalem Council, added a new thought to what happened when they were filled with the Holy Spirit. To the idea of being filled with power from God (1:8), Peter said the Holy Spirit also "purified their hearts by faith" (15:9).

So, the Scriptures indicate that the coming of the Holy Spirit into a person's life

    1. begins with waiting in prayerful anticipation

  2. comes by having faith that God wants to do something for the individual

  3. brings purity of heart and

  4. brings power for Christian service and witness

An Old Promise

We've spoken many times of God's original dreams, hopes, and plans for His children. We saw those dreams, hopes, and plans frustrated with sin's entrance into the picture. However, our Heavenly Father did not trash His dreams for His children. He found a way to bring us back to himself and restore us to His favor. The way was very costly in that He sacrificed His only Son Jesus Christ to accomplish it. That gives us a slight glimpse into how incredibly much He loved us.

The old sacrificial system left worshipers always searching spiritually for something more.

In the long history of God bringing His salvation plan to reality, He gave Moses and the Hebrew nation the Old Testament sacrificial system. We noted in chapter 4 how it showed people their sins and pointed them to God. However, it never removed the deep sense of guilt or left them with a spirit of freedom from sin. Rather, it left them in a ritualistic cycle that they repeated year after year, always searching spiritually for something deeper.

Even during the period of the Old Testament sacrificial system, God gave His prophets glorious promises and images of what would happen someday when His Holy Spirit arrived. The books of the prophets echo with many of those promises and images. Here are just a few to whet the appetites of God's followers about what they could expect.

Prophets Saw It Coming

Isaiah's vision of God's holiness, recorded in Isa. 6, changed his heart and life forever. But more than just calling him and his friends to righteous living, Isaiah glanced into the future to the day when God's Spirit would fill followers in spiritual ways. "For I will pour water on the thirsty land, and streams on the dry ground; I will pour out my Spirit on your offspring, and my blessing on your descendants" (44:3). No more spiritual dryness when the Holy Spirit comes! The prophet saw that He would come like long-awaited rain on parched soil. Those nomads of the desert knew the value of a good rain shower to the desert floor. They also anticipated the day when God would turn His dream into reality and rain showers of spiritual blessing on their parched souls.

The prophet Jeremiah experienced dark days as he watched his people forsake God and be exiled into foreign lands by their enemies. He watched them hauled off into captivity by the thousands. But he did not lose hope. He saw the day coming when God would write His wishes and desires for His people, not in rule books placed on library shelves, but down deep in followers' hearts. He saw the day of the Holy Spirit coming and predicted,

> "The time is coming," declares the LORD, "when I will make a new covenant with the house of Israel and with the house of Judah. It will not be like the covenant I made with their forefathers when I took them by the hand to lead them out of Egypt, because they broke my covenant, though I was a husband to them," declares the LORD. "This is the covenant I will make with the house of Israel after that time," declares the LORD. "I will put my law in their minds and write it on their hearts. I will be their God, and they will be my people" *(Jer. 31:31-33)*.

See the hunger of a loving Father to rebuild the relationship with His children? See the eagerness to start anew with a different plan? See the deep desire of God to create new family memories? The words may be a little different, but the idea remains the same as it had always been. The Father wanted to make things right between us.

Ezekiel lived at the same time as Jeremiah and watched his people turn from God and receive punishment from their enemies. And, like Jeremiah, he did not lose hope. He, too, saw hope for God's followers with the Holy Spirit's arrival. He imaged it like this,

> I will show the holiness of my great name, which has been profaned among the nations, the name you have profaned among them. Then the nations will know that I am the LORD, declares the Sovereign LORD, when I show myself holy through you before their eyes. . . . I will sprinkle clean water on you, and you will be clean; I will cleanse you from all your impurities and from all your idols. I will give you a new heart and put a new spirit in you; I will remove from you your heart of stone and give you a heart of flesh. And I will put my Spirit in you and move you to follow my decrees and be careful to keep my laws *(Ezek. 36:23, 25-27)*.

Note the imagery here: holiness revealed, no more profaning, a heart cleansing, a new heart, a new spirit, removal of a stony heart, and replacement with a warm heart. Like Jeremiah, Ezekiel saw the Spirit's inner presence bringing an internal awareness of God's will and plan for our lives.

Along with that He would bring the power to accomplish it. Notice that the holiness of God will be revealed to the world through us! What an awesome vision! People will see God and His holiness as they watch His family.

The prophet Joel also saw the fulfillment of God's promise to send us the Holy Spirit. Peter recognized Joel's vision coming to reality at Pentecost. That is why Peter quoted this passage in his Pentecost Day sermon. Hear Joel imagine that coming day,

> And afterward, I will pour out my Spirit on all people. Your sons and daughters will prophesy, your old men will dream dreams, your young men will see visions. Even on my servants, both men and women, I will pour out my Spirit in those days (Joel 2:28-29).

So, we see from these visions of God's prophets that God had been planning this special gift of the Holy Spirit for a long, long time. With each passing year, God's promised plan for His children became a little clearer. The prophets marveled as they received glimpses of it. What Jesus promised His disciples on the Mount of Olives just before His ascension simply restated an old promise that God had been making to His servants across the years. When He eventually fulfilled His promise, it proved to be just as glorious and wonderful as He had anticipated it would be.

God's Special Possession

The Holy Spirit cleansed them from sin and empowered their witness for God.

When the Holy Spirit entered the waiting believers' hearts, He cleansed them from sin and empowered their witness for God. This brought growth in the church. This new community of faith reminds us of another hope and dream that the Father had in the beginning. He always dreamed of having a group of followers who would separate themselves from other identities so they could be His special possession.

God shared His hope with Moses that the nation of Israel might be His special possession. "For you are a people holy to the LORD your God. The LORD your God has chosen you out of all the peoples on the face of the earth to be his people, his treasured possession" (Deut. 7:6).

Treasured possession. What an incredible thought! The Creator of a thousand galaxies across a million light-years most highly treasures His family members! Later in the book, God shared His vision again. "For you are a people holy to the LORD your God. Out of all the peoples on the face of the earth, the LORD has chosen you to be his treasured possession" (14:2). There it is again. The Father wants this so badly that He'll do anything to make it a reality.

History reveals that the nation of Israel never fulfilled God's dreams for them. They had a difficult time completely trusting Him during their desert wanderings after leaving Egyptian captivity. After they settled into the Promised Land they fell into cycles of losing their affection for God and drifting into living like their pagan neighbors. They got into deep trouble and eventually cried out for God's help. He restored them again and again, but they couldn't seem to break their old habits. They lacked something essential to fulfilling God's plan for their lives.

It looked at the time like the golden age of Israel may have arrived under the leadership of King David. This national leader had a heart for God. He did not rule perfectly, but he directed the nation toward God. Unfortunately, David's son and successor, Solomon, led his people back into their idolatrous ways. The kingdom soon divided into two separate nations that were conquered by their enemies. These enemies transported large numbers of Hebrew people into captivity again.

When they were released from their bondage, the leaders of Israel determined to never again fall into the idolatry trap. They said they had learned their bitter lesson. However, they did return to idolatry in an unexpected way. This time instead of worshiping carved objects, they paid idolatrous attention to their own religious rules. Hundreds of rules replaced warm, daily fellowship with God. Researchers estimate that people across the ages have created 35,000 rules to amplify the Ten Commandments. So, God's dreams for Israel remained unfulfilled as they bogged themselves in human-made rules.

When the church began to take shape after the miracles of Pentecost, God's hopes and dreams for a special people resurfaced. Peter saw God's special possession coming through the church. "But you are a chosen people, a royal priesthood, a holy nation, a people belonging to God, that you may declare the praises of him who called you out of darkness into his wonderful light" (1 Pet. 2:9). Peter's analysis of the Christian Church sounds a lot like God's hopes for a special people described in Deut. 7:6, doesn't it? In Deuteronomy God dreamed for a treasured possession. In Peter we see the dream brought to reality.

We see more reminders of the Father's special plans for His special creations. How did we get to be so special in His eyes? That's a mystery that will take us all eternity to understand. But until then, we can live in the daily blessing that we are indeed privileged by our Heavenly Father.

Full Circle

So now we've come full circle. We talked about God's original plan and the way we tarnished it. We saw how Christ made the sacrifice necessary to restore the family relationship. But, would forgiveness in Christ be more than turning over a new leaf and giving folks a fresh start? It should because folks in the Old Testament got fresh starts from God all the time, and the fresh starts never worked in the long run.

Now we've come full circle.

For example, on several occasions in Exodus and Judges, God wiped the slate clean and let His people start at ground zero. Unfortunately, they soon fell back into the same cycle of failures. They needed a helper to operate from the center of their being. If help could come from within, rather than just from trying to follow external laws, perhaps the failure cycle could be broken.

That's why Pentecost ranks so highly in salvation history. With Pentecost and the arrival of the Holy Spirit in a new relationship with believers came the possibility of God having His treasured possession—of a family living in vital relationship with Him. Can't you almost see it? Those hopes and dreams Father Creator had back at the hospital the first time He held Adam and Eve in His arms now have a new chance. It's been a long time in coming. But we're on to something now!

Fast Takes

1. The Holy Spirit's arrival at Pentecost brought fulfillment to the Father's promises.

2. Prophets throughout the Old Testament predicted how life would change when God's promised Spirit came to humanity.

3. The Holy Spirit cleansed believers from sin and empowered their witness for God.

4. Pentecost brought the possibility of God having His treasured possession—a family living in vital relationship with Him.

Think About This . . .

1. Why do you think Jesus went back to the Father before the Holy Spirit empowered the Church?

2. What role do you think gathering as a group played in their anticipation of the Holy Spirit's coming?

3. What role did praying and waiting play in the disciples' anticipation of the coming of the Holy Spirit?

4. What do the special symbols of Pentecost (wind, fire, and languages) say about what God wants to do in our lives today?

5. In what ways do we need purity and power just as the first disciples needed them?

6. In what ways did the Old Testament sacrificial system draw people toward God?

7. In what ways did the Old Testament sacrificial system fail in its purpose?

8. What did the Old Testament prophets see God doing in the future with the new contract He would make with His followers?

9. What could the Holy Spirit accomplish that the Old Testament sacrificial system could not accomplish?

10. How are Christians the special possession of God?

The person who knows that God is
the central fact of life,
feels the daily nearness of God,
sees the constant evidence of God's love,
offers self in gratitude to God,
is a transformed person.

6

THE TRANSFORMATION

Unrealized Dreams

Kevin attended our university several years ago. He came from a Christian home and grew up in a wonderful local church. He had all of the advantages of loving parents and good Christian role models in his home church. But, for whatever reason, Kevin arrived at our Christian university away from God and with a chip on his shoulder. He was out of sorts with himself and his world. He struggled spiritually throughout his college years.

He finally graduated with a degree in business and moved out to take his place in society. Where is Kevin today? Divorced, still dabbling in drugs, still missing a focus in life, still away from God. It's a sad picture, really. So much love and support from his parents; so little response from Kevin.

We know the reality; it happens all too often. Parents' hopes and dreams for their children go unrealized. Parents do their best to provide their children with everything needed to accomplish great things with their lives. But for one reason or another, the children decide not to strive for the goal.

Something Unusual Needed

If God's hopes and dreams for a special people had any chance of coming true, something unusual would be required to bring them to pass. God cast His vision for the nation of Israel, but they never really caught it. So, God wrote a new contract with a renewed hope of creating a special people; we find that new contract in the New Testament. It's the good news of new life in Jesus Christ. Jesus undid the damage of the garden fall, and He opened a new way for us to relate to God. The last

Jesus undid the damage of the garden fall, and He opened a new way for us to relate to God.

chapter focused on that new way made possible with the coming of the Holy Spirit at Pentecost.

Paul's discussion in Rom. 5:12—8:39 continues that thought. You might read this passage before you read the rest of this chapter. It will set the stage for all that follows.

Paul begins this passage by talking about our problem with the sin nature—that twist in our thinking toward self-preference. Adam and Eve's sinful choice threw all humanity out of balance with God and themselves (vv. 12-14). Christ came as a second Adam, exposed himself to the same temptations to sin, and obeyed God. He did what Adam and Eve did not do. He then went to the Cross to purchase our salvation.

Thus, Christ undid Adam and Eve's damage. That is what led Paul to say, "For just as through the disobedience of the one man the many were made sinners, so also through the obedience of the one man the many will be made righteous" (v. 19). The grace and gift of God in Christ Jesus destroys sin's dominion over us (vv. 20-21).

Once sin's power over us is broken, we are freed to live a new kind of life. How is this possible? By identifying with Christ in His crucifixion, our old life of sin dies. The act of baptism symbolizes this death as we are buried in a water grave and raised to new spiritual life. In this way our old sinful self, unregenerate and away from God, is destroyed. It no longer has power over us. The resurrection life of Jesus Christ working through us replaces it (6:1-10). Paul has no notions of destroying a believer's identity. The individual does not die. Rather, Paul means to say the self-sovereignty of living outside of God's full control dies.

The death of the old to make way for the new reminds me of something that happened this year with my best friend's lawn. Gary's neighbor has a different type of grass in his yard than Gary does. It's a different shade of green, has a different type blade, and grows much faster. This spring grass seeds from the neighbor's yard blew into Gary's yard and grew everywhere. The foreign grass made Gary's lawn look terrible. He only had one choice: spray a grass killer on the infected areas of his lawn and start over with new seed. After he did that, his lawn looked great. The same must happen with us. God must destroy the old nature to enable His new nature to emerge.

God's Dreams Become Reality

With this background of Adam's failure and Christ's success clearly in view, Paul moves on in Rom. 6 to a wonderful picture of God's efforts to fulfill His hopes and dreams in us. Since Christ, by His death on the Cross, undid the garden damage, then spiritually speaking, we're back to square one with God's original plan. It can now be realized in us. Paul's discussion weaves back and forth between what God does for us and what He expects us to do in response to His actions.

First, Paul says, "Count yourselves dead to sin but alive to God in Christ Jesus" (v. 11). That means we are to live as if God's new life really is at work in us. Why? Because it is. Make the possibility a reality in your mind. Does that mean simply believing in positive thinking? Does it ask us to believe something that is not true? No, it means believing in the power of God to do as He promised and really change us.

> *Live as if God's new life really is at work in us. Why? Because it is.*

Next, we are to "not let sin reign in [our] mortal bodies so that [we] obey its evil desires" (v. 12). Christ has broken the power of that reign through His death on the Cross. We identify ourselves with His death. God creates the possibility; we respond by living the reality.

Since we once chose to sin, we can now choose not to sin. God doesn't take the power to sin away from us; He breaks the power of sin's desire. It's a matter of living with a made-up mind. A mind that's made a decision goes a long way in keeping sin out of our pockets.

Further, "Do not offer the parts of your body to sin, as instruments of wickedness, but rather offer yourselves to God, as those who have been brought from death to life; and offer the parts of your body to him as instruments of righteousness" (v. 13). We leave the old sinful lifestyle behind; we move away and leave no forwarding address. We replace that old lifestyle with full devotion to God. This results in lives characterized by right living. Like Davy Crockett said, "Always be sure you're right, then go ahead."[1]

God's grace replaces our bondage to the law. This free grace does not mean we are free to go on sinning. Never! Paul says grace does not offer freedom to sin; it offers freedom from sin. We become slaves to whatever controls us. Our old lives meant control by bondage to sin's habits. Our new master, then, is Christ; our new slavery is righteousness (vv. 14-18).

Where does this new contract with God lead? Paul gives the answer in verse 19. It is "righteousness leading to holiness." That's where Paul's argument has been leading all along—a renewal of God's dream leads to holiness. He continues in verse 22 to say, "The benefit you reap leads to holiness, and the result is eternal life."

Eternal life begins the moment we accept Christ as Savior. It continues to surge through our veins both here on earth and in the timelessness of heaven. As Johann Kaspar Lavater said, "Act well at the moment and you have performed a good action to all eternity."[2]

All along the way, on this side of heaven's door, we grow in our relationship with God. That growth takes place on the road of holiness.

Crucified with Christ

Paul expands his thought on identifying with Christ's death and resurrection in Gal. 2:20 where he said, "I have been crucified with Christ and I no longer live, but Christ lives in me. The life I live in the body, I live by faith in the Son of God, who loved me and gave himself for me."

Dead people have no desires.

Paul's old life of sin and hunger for sin's pleasures died. His self-preference for his own ways also died with Christ. As A. W. Tozer put it, "To be crucified means, first, the man on the cross is faced in only one direction; second, he is not going back; and third, he has no further plans of his own."[3]

Dead people have no desires. You can hold sin's most enticing pleasures right under their noses, and they will feel no desire. So, with the old life gone, what is left? Only the will and desire of Christ.

What made this a reality in Paul's daily life? His faith in Christ as he realized Christ's love for him and the sacrifice made on the Cross.

Do Not Conform

In Rom. 6:11-14 Paul discusses counting ourselves dead to sin but alive to God; he also urges us to not offer the parts of our body to sin. Paul adds another symbol to this thought in 12:1-2. It's his discussion of a living sacrifice. He says,

Therefore, I urge you, brothers, in view of God's mercy, to offer your bodies as living sacrifices, holy and pleasing to God—this is your spiritual act of worship. Do not conform any longer to the pattern of this world, but be transformed by the renewing of your mind. Then you will be able to test and approve what God's will is—his good, pleasing and perfect will.

We discussed the concept of offering ourselves to God in chapter 4. We call our offer consecration. In consecration, we lay ourselves on God's altar just as people in the Old Testament laid sacrifices on the altars of the Tabernacle and Temple. Gifts brought to the altar in the Old Testament had to be spotless and without blemish.

We're neither spotless nor unblemished, but we do have the Holy Spirit living with us, so He makes our consecration to the Father possible. We offer back to Him the new life He gives us.

Paul says we present ourselves once and for all to God. When he says we offer our bodies, he means we offer every part of our being—body, soul, mind, and strength—to God. Giving God all of the keys to all of the rooms of our heart illustrates this effort.

My elderly pastor used to say, "We sign our name on the dotted line at the bottom of a blank sheet of paper." That is, we give Him everything of which we are aware and everything that remains in the shadows of the future. He fills in the blank page as He sees fit.

The Holy Spirit makes our consecration to the Father possible.

Let us now explore Paul's notion of not conforming to the pattern of this world. Paul is not speaking of the world in terms of nature with earth, sea, and sky. No criticism of Hawaii here!

He is talking about the system of thought that does things its own way, or worse yet, Satan's way. It puts self first and centers the universe around personal motivations. It manifests itself in self-will, self-love, self-trust, and self-exaltation. It seeks pleasure, power, position, and whatever else it wants. It places its own needs over others' needs.

How does a worldly mind-set manifest itself in daily life? These characteristics show up among Christians and non-Christians alike, both in the business world and in the church. We can demonstrate these attitudes toward God and other people. The following is not an exhaustive list, but I think you will get the point!

1. Self-centered: Acting as if the earth and all other planets in this universe revolve around you.

2. Self-assertive: Moving to the front of the line because you deserve to be first; having to win every table game.

3. Self-deprecating: Calling undue attention to yourself by putting yourself down in order to get others to praise you.

4. Conceited: Acting as if you are God's gift to humanity.

5. Self-indulgent: Looking primarily after your own wants and needs.

6. Self-pleasing: Making sure your family or group eats where you want to eat and watches the television program you want to watch—every time.

7. Self-seeking: Being so in love with yourself that your primary responsibility in life is to assure your own happiness.

8. Self-pity: Feeling sorry for yourself because you are so deprived, overweight, underweight, plagued, or whatever else darkens your world.

9. Defensive: Always making excuses to justify your behavior.

10. Self-sufficiency: Living as if you need no one else's help, not even God's.

11. Self-consciousness: Being so concerned about how you look or the impression you make on others that you accomplish little else; always worrying about what other people think.

12. Self-preoccupied: Being so focused on your own interests and needs that you are not aware of the world around you.

13. Self-introspective: Going around all day with your finger on your psychological, emotional, or spiritual pulse and monitoring every wavelength that passes through your brain.

14. Self-righteous: Getting blessed at the incredible blessing and contribution you are to God's work and being proud of your good example.

15. Self-glorying: Calling attention to your ministry and spiritual accomplishments and amazing even yourself at just how good you are.

16. Self-proclaiming: Announcing to everyone that you are God's answer to folks' prayers and declaring your ways to be God's wishes in a particular situation.

17. Self-made: Being proud of the fact that no one gave you money or support in helping you get where you are today.

What is the result of this pattern of thinking and living? It damages and destroys relationships with family and friends. It short-circuits concern for others. It ultimately results in loneliness and unfulfillment. It leaves a wake of evil and corruption. Satan told Eve, "You will not die." He lied. His pattern of thinking always leads to death.

But Be Transformed

When we offer ourselves to God and reject Satan's worldly ways, we save ourselves a truckload of heartache and grief. Further, we become candidates for Him to transform us from the inside out. That is, He transforms our mind, which results in transformed lifestyle. This new lifestyle honors God as it seeks to do His will.

The concept of transformation that Paul uses in this passage refers to what happens when a caterpillar changes from crawling in the dirt into a butterfly that takes wing for the sky. The Father transforms us with the same power source He used to raise Jesus from the dead. That's some high voltage!

The resurrection power of Jesus Christ flowing through our being reorients our thinking, our value system, our priorities, our motivations, and our desires. It completely renovates our personal system of thinking and living. This thorough, radical, universal power surge of resurrection energy transforms our mind, which brings an outward lifestyle change. By the way, this same concept of transformation occurred on the Mount of Transfiguration when Jesus shined with the radiance of His eternal glory.

We obviously are not transformed by our own efforts and personal energy source. It's too miraculous for that. Rather, the Holy Spirit of God transforms us in daily living as we consecrate ourselves to Him and let Him change us. This is what Paul meant in 2 Cor. 3:18 when he said, "And we, who with unveiled faces all reflect the Lord's glory, are being transformed into his likeness with ever-increasing glory, which comes from the Lord, who is the Spirit."

> *The Holy Spirit of God transforms us in daily living as we consecrate ourselves to Him and let Him change us.*

Consecration or Surrender?

Sometimes I hear people refer to our consecration as a surrender. They encourage believers to surrender to God, so He can take them to a new level of spiritual commitment. While we do offer ourselves to God in a new way, the word *surrender* misses the point. *Surrender* describes what an enemy does when conquered. It conjures images of white flags waving in the air or of arms raised high.

Our consecration to God is not with raised arms or white flags, though we may need to surrender from any struggle we experience when we realize the implications of giving God full control. Consecration more properly suggests a loving child offering a homemade gift to a parent. The gift and the wrapping paper may not be expensive; the wrapping technique may not be perfect. But the goal of the child's heart is to present something of himself or herself.

Salvation is God's gift to us; consecration is our gift to God. In our consecration, we offer ourselves—warts and all—to our Heavenly Father with the intention of Him using us as He wishes.

I mention warts because all of us have flaws and blemishes that cause us to be less than perfect. Sometimes consecration becomes difficult because we feel we have talents and abilities that may be wasted if given fully to God. I see this occasionally with bright students at our university who fear a complete consecration might require them to change their career plans from one with high income potential, to a minister, with a low income potential.

Sometimes relatives of these students have more trouble with a child's consecration than the child has. Just this year a grandmother told me she was grieved that her grandson, a premed senior, was trading his medical school plans for full-time ministry.

God sees infinitely more potential and ability in us than we see in ourselves.

More often than not, however, consecration becomes difficult because we feel we have nothing to offer God. Our talents and abilities, by our own estimation, rank somewhere between slim and none. We look at our dysfunctional relationships, failed attempts at different ventures, infirmities, and doubts. We hesitate to offer ourselves to God because we cannot locate anything worth presenting. We see only warts and blemishes.

God sees infinitely more potential and ability in us than we see in ourselves. One miracle of His grace is His talent for taking the little we think we have to offer and multiplying it into significant accomplishment for His kingdom. He works in us much like Jesus worked with the young boy's lunch during one of His teaching sessions. He used five biscuits and two little fish to cater a banquet for 5,000 families. Now that's stretching the groceries!

For reasons known only to Him, God chooses to build His kingdom through the efforts of one- and two-talent people. Look around the church. You won't see many megatalented people among us. Most of us can sing, speak, work with children, mow the grass, or cook a meal for a needy family. Few of us do a variety of things well. But God uses us all.

I think I know why. As Paul put it, "For it is by grace you have been saved, through faith—and this not from yourselves, it is the gift of God—not by works, so that no one can boast" (Eph. 2:8-9).

Boasting becomes impossible when we realize God accomplishes the good work that flows from our efforts. Only He deserves the praise and glory. So, He doesn't ask how many talents we possess; He asks for our faithfulness. Like my dad used to say, "A dedicated man with a rusty wrench can do more than a lazy man with all the tools in the shop."

All God asks of us is a willing heart, open to Him. If we let Him crucify our self-sovereign stronghold, we give Him the room He needs to transform our character. He only asks for our offer; He renews our mind with His miraculous transformation.

The conclusion of Paul's thoughts in Rom. 12:2 returns us to the fulfillment of God's original dream for us. That is, we will know and live God's will, "His good, pleasing and perfect will." What an incredible proud-parent dream God has for us!

Fast Takes

1. Christ undid Adam and Eve's damage; now we are freed to live a new kind of life.

2. Now, we're back to square one with God's original plan.

3. In consecration we lay ourselves on God's altar just as people in the Old Testament laid sacrifices on the altars of the Tabernacle and Temple.

4. Worldly thinking refers to the system of thought that does things its own way, or worse yet, Satan's way.

5. God transforms our mind, which results in transformed lifestyle; He uses the same power source He used to raise Jesus from the dead.

6. God sees infinitely more potential and ability in us than we see in ourselves.

Think About This . . .

1. Do you know anyone like Kevin, who did not realize his parents' hopes and dreams?

2. Why do you think children sometimes decide not to strive for a higher goal?

3. What did Jesus do different from Adam and Eve when tempted with sinful choices?

4. How is Paul's admonition in Rom. 6:11, to count ourselves dead to sin, different from wishful thinking?

5. How is our consecration like the Old Testament sacrifices? How is it different?

6. How does the Holy Spirit work in us to make our consecration possible?

7. Give examples of the various types of selfish thinking you see around you every day.

8. How does God transform our minds?

9. How can our consecration actually help us have a more realistic understanding of ourselves and our abilities?

10. Why is it impossible for a person sanctified by God to boast?

7

THE HELPER

Holiness and the Holy Spirit

The Bible makes a clear connection between God's holiness and our holiness. He is; we should be. However, we must never deceive ourselves into thinking that this connection is as easy to realize as imitating the actions of a leader in a children's game such as follow-the-leader. We've all played those games in which we watch the leader and then do exactly what he or she is doing.

Imitating God is different from imitating a game leader for several reasons. First, it's natural for God to live a holy life; it's in His nature to do so. He just does what comes naturally. He defines the very concept of holiness itself.

Second, God has all the power He needs to do exactly what He desires to do. No gap exists between God's wishes and His ability to fulfill them. Third, God is not weakened by the damage and effects of sin.

Our pursuit of holiness is limited in each of these ways. Human nature's automatic response urges us to pursue our own desires, to look out for number one—me. Preoccupation with self-interest runs counter to pursuing God's definition of holiness.

The gap that exists between our best intentions and our ability to carry them out creates another problem. How often have I wanted to do something lofty but didn't accomplish it because of spiritual or emotional weakness? The good intentions in my head don't always translate into good actions.

I must also come to terms with the fact that I live in a fallen world damaged by sin. I have a personal history also damaged by my past sinful choices and their consequences. What's more, I live with a fallen nature. I see bad examples all around me and hear daily reports of others making sinful choices. Though I wouldn't always admit it, sometimes these bad examples tempt me. At the same time, I look at my past mistakes and wonder if the baggage of the haunting memories will ever go away.

"Who am I kidding?" I cry. "I've been too bad for God to make me holy." All of these factors contribute to my inability to imitate God's holy example.

How, then, can we consider God's holiness and pursue any effort at following this example? This exists as a possibility in our lives only as the Holy Spirit helps us.

Life and Relationship

We must constantly remember: holiness is more than an abstract concept, more than a theory to be proved, more than a doctrine to be dissected. Holiness is a way of living made possible through a personal relationship with God. Life and relationship replace letter and law. And that changes the whole complexion of our discussion. So, when we talk about holiness we must explore our lovelife with God.

Holiness is a way of living made possible through a personal relationship with God.

God makes personal relationship with Him possible by the ministry of the Holy Spirit who lives and works in us. Our first encounter with the Holy Spirit does not come when we begin to search for a life of holiness.

He first intersects our lives when we are deep in sin and running from God. He first brings conviction to our hearts. He awakens us to the error of our ways. And He makes us feel bad about it. He hits the warning button on our conscience, which we usually ignore as long as we can. But He eventually piques frustration and unfulfillment to the point where we desperately seek relief.

The Holy Spirit creates spiritual crisis in our lives. We respond to His call by coming as rebels in surrender to God's love. When we reach the end of our rope, we're ready to accept whatever He has for us. He replaces our pain and defeat with new birth. We become new creations in Christ. As Paul says, "The old has gone, the new has come!" (2 Cor. 5:17).

This new life comes through the work of the Holy Spirit. He connects us to the Father and the Son in our new spiritual relationship with our Creator. So, the Holy Spirit works to bring us to the Father and give us His gift of new spiritual life long before we look to Him for a deeper walk with God. As Alfred, Lord Tennyson put it, "Closer is He than breathing, and nearer than hands and feet."[1]

The Paraclete

Everything Jesus said about the Holy Spirit tells us He is a person—not an impersonal force. Modern movies talk about "The Force" as an impersonal power for all of us to tap into and draw strength from. We only need to recognize its presence and use it.

Not so with the Holy Spirit. Neither is He a thing. I often hear people refer to the Spirit with the pronoun "it." They urge us to seek "it." Actually they are referring to some sort of religious experience, I think. But in so doing they depreciate the personhood of the Spirit. How demeaning. Would you speak to someone about your pastor by saying, "It drives a black car." Of course not. Neither is the Holy Spirit an "it." He is a person like you and me.

> **The Holy Spirit is not "The Force"!**

Jesus taught us most of what we know about the Holy Spirit in John 14—17. This passage contains the five Paraclete Sayings of Jesus about the coming of the Holy Spirit. These five sayings are found in 14:15-18; 14:26-27; 15:26-27; 16:7-11; and 16:13-14. *Paraclete* is the Greek word usually translated "Comforter, Counselor, Advocate, or Helper." The literal meaning is "one called alongside."

Paraclete pictures a lawyer who stands beside us in a courtroom. He both supports us by standing at our side and speaks to the judge and jury on our behalf. He knows the law better than we know it and argues our case for us. He stands with us as our Advocate and Friend, giving us the best representation possible.

In looking at all of the English words translated from the Greek word *Paraclete,* we gain new insight into the Holy Spirit's ministry. As our Counselor, He listens carefully to our situation or need, then gives meaningful advice. As our Comforter, He analyzes our weakness and provides His strength; He says just what we need to soothe our hurts. As our Advocate, He defends us against Satan's attacks and arguments, counsels us on how to live our lives, and advises us in making decisions. As our Helper, He goes beyond advice to providing actual power to carry out and put the advice into action.

Another Counselor

In John 14:15-18 Jesus refers to the Holy Spirit as "another Counselor." Jesus is our first Counselor, but He was about to leave His disciples. We must continue to love and obey Jesus in order for Him to send us this new Counselor. Jesus gives us a clue to His relationship with the Holy Spirit in verse 18 when He tells His disciples, "I will come to you." On Good Friday, Jesus' enemies walked confidently down the hill of Calvary, washed the dirt and blood from their hands, and tried to forget the whole matter. Surely they had successfully silenced another religious fanatic.

"I will come to you."
—Jesus

But something went terribly wrong with their plan. For today, millions of people around the world live in daily communion with Him. They speak to Him, listen to Him, consult Him, are guided by Him, and draw daily inspiration from Him. They live because He lives.

How? The Holy Spirit brings us the living Christ. Without the Spirit, Jesus would only be an impersonal memory. He would be just another page in an old scrapbook. His words would be remembered like those of Confucius, Aristotle, or Muhammad.

I've seen shrines to these lifeless people around the world. One of the most moving spiritual experiences of my entire life happened in Red Square, Moscow, as I visited the open casket of Nikolai Lenin. I stood close enough to almost touch the lifeless body of this man who died in 1924. I thought about how he masterminded the communist revolution with its strong commitment to atheism. My heart leaped for joy. Lenin is dead—the revolution is dead—Jesus lives!

The good news is—if you are a Christian, the Creator of the universe lives and works in your life through the Holy Spirit. As Paul put it, "Christ in you, the hope of glory" (Col. 1:27). That is because when He left His disciples, Jesus said, "I will come to you."

The Teacher

Jesus left us with His preaching ministry, His parables, His sayings, His teachings, His miracles, His lifestyle, His example, and His command to evangelize the world. How on earth can we do all of that? How can we live up to the standard He set for us? How can we follow all of His teachings? How can we reproduce His ministry in our world? How can we be His light in the darkness?

Talk about unrealistic expectations! We can't do all of this by our own strength and effort. If we read the Bible or pay close attention in Sunday School class or listen carefully to the sermon and try to live the Christian life in our own strength, we will experience nothing but frustration and defeat. We will have lofty ideals but will not be able to translate them into practical living. That was the problem with the Old Testament law. It miscarried at producing faithful children of God because it provided no internal power source. It depended almost completely on human efforts.

That's why we need the Holy Spirit. He creates the essential link between lofty goals and holy living. Our striving is not what accomplishes anything of lasting value; it's what He does through us that counts. So, learning to know Him better and opening ourselves more fully to Him pave the way to Christian holiness.

We can attend Sunday School class, morning worship, and week-night Bible study. We can read our Bibles faithfully. But all of our efforts only frustrate us unless He teaches us. Jesus said, "The Holy Spirit . . . will teach you all things" (John 14:26).

Higher education is experiencing great days with continuing education. Middle-aged adults are returning to college in record numbers. But that's nothing new. The Holy Spirit has had a continuing education program in place since Pentecost.

> *The Holy Spirit creates the essential link between lofty goals and holy living.*

Late in his life Paul said all he knew about Christ only reached first base to what could be known. In one of his last prayers he prayed, "I want to know Christ" (Phil. 3:10). That must be our heart's cry: to know Christ. That only happens as we get in the flow of the Holy Spirit. That's one of the reasons holiness offers such hope—it helps us know Christ better.

Wanda, my previous secretary at the university where I work, once became frustrated with the books, coats, wastepaper, and used foam cups she found lying around the office at the end of the day. She placed a little sign by the coffeemaker that read, "I'm not your mother." Everyone got the point.

That's one reason God gave us mothers. To remind us of what we already know to do. God knows that we need to be told again and again. That's why He gave us mothers, and it's why He gives us the Holy Spirit. Jesus said, "[He] will remind you of everything I have said to you" (John 14:26).

John Wesley once preached a sermon at Newmarket that mightily moved the people. Someone remarked about the great impact he was having on the crowds. He responded, "Perhaps they may remember it—a week!"[2] How quickly we forget!

So we need to be open to the Holy Spirit's reminding ministry. How often has the Spirit spoken to me but the seed fell on the stony ground of a preoccupied mind or an insensitive spirit. He came back later and reminded me of what He once taught me. That's evidence of the importance of holiness—we must stay close to God's Spirit so He can remind us of what we so easily forget.

Jesus closed His last evening with His disciples by saying, "Peace I leave with you; my peace I give you" (v. 27). If we're looking for the Holy Spirit to come to us in a great cloud of signs and wonders, we've missed the point. If we're waiting for an electrical charge to surge through our bodies and souls at 440 volts, we've missed the focus of holiness and the Holy Spirit.

During my first year as religion professor, I prayed with one of my students during a revival service. After praying for a few minutes, I asked him what he wanted God to do for him. He said he wanted the Holy Spirit to fill him. We prayed a while longer, but he said God had not met the need of his heart.

Probing his expectations, I discovered he expected to feel a great surge of power go through him like you feel when you get shocked with a faulty extension cord. He said until he felt that, he couldn't believe God's Spirit was living and abiding in his heart. Unfortunately, his expectations blinded him to God's ability to satisfy His heart hunger. He left church that day feeling defeated.

I know that story sounds humorous and sad at the same time, but it characterizes the misunderstandings we sometimes attach to holiness. I fear some people hunger more for an "experience" or a "feeling" than they do for a deeper relationship with God. Holiness is not a feeling; it's a vital connection with the Spirit of God.

God doesn't come to us in prepackaged experiences that everyone senses in the same way. Neither does He always work in sequentially numbered steps that we can chart on a graph. That frustrates record keepers. It shouldn't. He comes to us according to the level of our understanding and need. We each testify to God's work in us a little differently. The most common description I hear from my friends sounds like Jesus' promise in this verse: a deep sense of peace.

When the Holy Spirit comes and purifies our hearts by faith and gives us power for service, a struggle ends, a stress is relieved, a peace fills our entire being. We often refer to this peace as the witness of the Holy Spirit. He speaks to our hearts that He has accepted our consecration and sanctified us. As I said, different people describe it in different ways. Ultimately we rest in the fact that God has done what He said He would do. As Scripture reminds us, "Because by one sacrifice he has made perfect forever those who are being made holy. The Holy Spirit also testifies to us about this" (Heb. 10:14-15).

"Those who obey his commands live in him, and he in them. And this is how we know that he lives in us: We know it by the Spirit he gave us" (1 John 3:24).

The Witness

In the third Paraclete Saying Jesus refers to the Holy Spirit as the Witness. "When the Counselor comes, whom I will send to you from the Father, the Spirit of truth who goes out from the Father, he will testify about me" (John 15:26). That is an important work of the Holy Spirit: to testify to the world about the life, ministry, and salvation plan of Christ. He is called "the Spirit of truth" because He tells us about the One who is "the truth" (14:6).

We hear a great deal about Christians witnessing. It seems like a daunting task. Jesus commands, "And you also must testify, for you have been with me from the beginning" (15:27). The work of the Holy Spirit within us carries the secret for the success of this command. We don't witness by our own strength or power. We witness as "the Witness" lives in us and works through us. We follow His lead and say what He prompts us to say.

Convicting the World

Jesus' fourth Paraclete Saying tells us, "When he [the Holy Spirit] comes, he will convict the world of guilt in regard to sin and righteousness and judgment" (16:8). We spoke earlier in this chapter of how the Holy Spirit first intersected our lives when we were lost rebels. He brought us conviction. He talked to us about our sin, about the need to live righteous lives, and about the coming day of judgment. This conviction brought us to a point of frustration that demanded a remedy. At the time, it seemed terrible. However, in looking back, we see the wonderful love of God drawing us through His Spirit. This drawing love resulted in our salvation and our love affair with God.

The Guide

In the final Paraclete Saying, Jesus promises a Guide who will guide us into all truth. As in previous Paraclete Sayings, Jesus indicates that the message of the Holy Spirit will be from the mouth of Jesus Christ. The Father, Son, and Spirit work so closely together that none speaks separately of the other. "He will speak only what he hears" (v. 13). He also tells us of things "yet to come" (v. 13).

This could refer to the Spirit giving us insights into what lies ahead in the future, as He did with the apostle John in the Book of Revelation. More than likely, however, it probably refers to showing us what is ahead for us and how to prepare for living the Christian life every day.

Jesus brought glory to His Father during His earthly ministry. In this passage we see the Spirit bringing glory to the Son (v. 14). The Son takes spiritual insight on living from His Father; the Spirit takes this insight and passes it on to us. What an incredible privilege we enjoy through the ministry of the Holy Spirit!

Greater Workers

At the beginning of His discussion of the Holy Spirit in John 14 Jesus made a powerful prediction. He said, "Anyone who has faith in me will do what I have been doing. He will do even greater things than these, because I am going to the Father" (v. 12).

> *Greater works than Jesus? I don't think so!*

What a mouthful. Greater works than Jesus? I don't think so! Not by ourselves.

However, look at the Early Church. It was a little group of ragtag, bickering, carnal, self-seeking, hiding followers who were scared of their own shadows. And yet, they turned the Roman Empire on its ear! Do you think they did that because of a well-organized committee meeting Peter held or a church-growth seminar that John conducted?

No way! Neither their organization nor their methods produced their success. Their trade secret? The Holy Spirit of God working through them.

The same is true for us. Let's face it, if building the Church depends on our efforts and plans, the whole thing will wash down the river with the next hard rain. But it doesn't. God's work didn't depend on the early disciples, and it doesn't depend on us. He works as we depend on Him. He's the source of power; we're the vessels. The Church today has far too much struggle, far too much effort, far too much strain, pull, and tug. What we need to see in large quantity is people trusting in the Spirit of God to build His Church through our openness. Holiness means opening ourselves for God to pour through us.

The Life-Giving Flow

We must always remember holiness is not about an experience in itself. It's not about a doctrine in abstraction. It's not about numbered steps toward God. It's about close, personal fellowship with God's Spirit. Nothing else in our spirituality makes sense without that.

Consider the possibility. We can love the Lord, dedicate our allegiance to Him, come to church regularly, teach a Sunday School class, serve on a church committee or the church board—and miss the life-giving flow of God's Spirit who energizes the entire Christian life. The Holy Spirit wants to change that perspective. He wants to energize all we do. He's the Helper we need.

Fast Takes

1. We can pursue the holiness of a holy God only as the Holy Spirit helps us.

2. Life and relationship replace letter and law in a life of holiness.

3. The Holy Spirit comes to us as a Counselor, Teacher, Witness, Convictor, and Guide.

4. The work Jesus called us to imitate from His ministry can only be done with the help of the Holy Spirit.

5. Holiness means opening ourselves for God to pour through us.

Think About This . . .

1. What factors contribute to your feelings of inadequacy at imitating God's holiness?

2. Why is your love life with God so essential to a holy life?

3. Recall the way God's Spirit put you under conviction before your conversion. How did you feel?

4. Why is it improper to refer to the Holy Spirit as a religious experience? Why do people do it so often?

5. List the ways the Holy Spirit helps us the way a lawyer helps us.

6. List the ways the Holy Spirit has comforted you in your Christian walk.

7. List the ways the Holy Spirit has taught or reminded you in your Christian walk.

8. List the ways the Holy Spirit has helped you share your faith in Christ.

9. List the ways the Holy Spirit has brought conviction to you since you became a Christian.

10. List the ways the Holy Spirit has guided your spiritual life.

In my heart there is only one vacant seat.
It is for God and nobody else.
—*Mother Teresa*[1]

8

E T A

Estimated Time of Arrival (ETA)

No doubt you've heard the maxim, "Timing is everything." It refers to the importance of good timing in activities—whether you're telling a joke, paying bills, or executing a basketball play.

I'll never forget my encounter with timing a few years ago in the Dallas-Fort Worth International Airport. I sat at the airport gate one Friday morning with 22 college students and 2 other sponsors waiting to board the next leg of our Work and Witness trip from Kansas City to Georgetown, Guyana.

Our itinerary took us from Kansas City to Dallas to Miami to Port of Spain, Trinidad, for an overnight stay at a Bible college, then on to Georgetown on Saturday morning. Every connection required careful timing as we worked with the ETA of each arrival and departure. So far our team remained right on schedule.

"Frank Moore, please step to the desk at Gate 24," broadcast over the loudspeaker system. I approached the desk. The gate agent said, "Mr. Moore, you have a group of 25 on this flight to Miami, don't you?"

"Yes, I do."

"Sir, we have a problem with this flight being oversold by exactly 25 seats. I will give you travel vouchers worth $25,000 if you will take your group on the following Miami flight leaving in about 2 hours." Without batting an eye but with a sick feeling running through my body, I choked out, "I can't do it. Our ETA into Miami gives us just enough time to make our connection to South America. If we miss that flight, we'll throw our group arrangements off in three cities over the next 24 hours."

The gate agent then went public with his offer and 25 passengers quickly lined up to receive $1,000 each! That's one time I wished timing wasn't everything. Not only does timing apply to travel arrangements, but it's also important in our relationship with God.

Now or Later?

Folks who study the Bible and Christian experience agree that sanctification deserves our careful attention and study. The Bible speaks often of it; Christians who are fully open to God's direction for their lives speak of His sanctifying work in them. Hence, few people question the validity of sanctification, though many question the details of it.

One of the most frequently asked questions relates to God's timetable for accomplishing sanctification in our lives. Does He work in a moment of time or does He work over a lifetime? The answer is yes to both questions. Does He sanctify us from the very beginning of our Christian walk or after we consecrate ourselves fully to Him? Again, the answer is yes.

The answer to those questions cannot be described by saying it's either this way or that way; more properly it's both this way and that way.

I also know holiness folks tend to side off into two camps. Camp No. 1 emphasizes the moment in time when we consecrate all to God and He accepts our offer. Camp No. 2 emphasizes the slow freight train that carries our incremental growth.

I know that sounds like the response of a smooth-tongued politician.

Sorry, you simply cannot emphasize one to the exclusion of the other. Those in Camp No. 1 tend to fall into the trap of getting frozen in two experiences. Those in Camp No. 2 tend to fall into the trap of getting lost on a road without mile markers or signs. The Christian journey becomes one big process. So, we must tear down the fence between the two camps and emphasize the good features of each. I know that sounds like the response of a smooth-tongued politician. How can everybody be right?

Sanctification's ETA

Honestly, what can we expect on the ETA of sanctification? I'm afraid you can't call the pastor and get a definitive arrival time the way you can call the airport for today's flight arrivals. It's far more complex than that, though ETAs for airliners are pretty complex too!

For one thing, spiritual development occurs in people, not machines. We cannot package it the way we package instructions for programming your VCR. We've all had different backgrounds, upbringings, educations, and experiences. We also all have different personalities. And people interpret scripture passages about sanctification differently.

We don't have time to explore every detail of the different interpretations of sanctification passages. Let's look at the central features of a few of the views.

1. *Sanctification happens after a person dies.*

This interpretation sees heaven as a perfect place. In order to keep us from polluting it the moment we step foot through the doorway, this view holds that God must do something to make us holy or fit for our new perfect environment.

Since believers fail to score perfectly on spiritual maturity tests right up until the day they die, then it stands to reason that God must accomplish His holy work in us *after* we die. I call this the quantum leap view because we close our eyes in death, take a giant step through the door of eternity, and open our eyes clothed in perfection.

I call this the quantum leap view.

This view makes sense, but it's not biblical. The hundreds of references to sanctification in the Bible speak of it as a present reality, not pie in the sky by and by. This view also takes me off the hook of living a righteous life while on earth. Why strive for holiness now when I can simply wait for God's quantum leap work following my death?

2. *Sanctification happens just before a person dies.*

This interpretation sees us growing incrementally in God's sanctifying grace throughout life. Sometime just before our earthly departure, God graduates us from the growth process and grants us sanctification. This prepares us to enter heaven's perfection. Because it happens at the time of death, we call it "dying grace."

Such a view sounds logical, but it has no biblical basis. Nothing in Scripture indicates that God withholds His gift of sanctification until moments before we die. This view also has problems in life's arena. What about people involved in sudden automobile or airplane accidents? Does God grant believers this grace in the microseconds before death's blow? What of those who slip into a coma and never regain consciousness? Does God provide this grace to unconscious believers? What about people whose illnesses reach a terminal stage, so they pray for and receive "dying grace," then recover from their illness? Does God take back His special sanctifying grace or let the individual keep it until death revisits?

This interpretation has biblical and logical problems. All explanations of dying grace make it sound automatic rather than a gift received from God by faith, which is the biblical notion. It certainly does not help believers in the daily grind of life, since it comes only in time for the journey home. It more nearly resembles a bon voyage gift received before a long trip.

3. *Sanctification happens instantaneously at the time God forgives us of our sins and gives us new birth.*

This interpretation joins the new birth and sanctification as twin gifts of God granted simultaneously like a coin with two sides. Hence, when a person asks God for forgiveness of sin and accepts Christ as Savior, he or she receives regeneration-sanctification. This view does not see believers growing in holiness throughout life but simply living within the gift granted at the beginning of the Christian life.

If this interpretation represents a biblical position, then all of the Bible's appeals to sanctification and holiness must have been made to sinners. It also fails to explain how sinners can offer themselves to God in consecration as a spiritual act of worship while in rebellion against God.

The problem with this interpretation resides not with God's inability to grant us multiple levels of grace at one time; the problem resides with our inability to comprehend multiple levels of understanding at the same time.

Full sanctification in an instant would be like presenting a newborn with a stroller, tricycle, scooter, bicycle, and car all at the same time.

God deals with us at every stage of our spiritual journey according to the level of our comprehension. Because we tend to master one concept at a time, God works with us according to our developmental ability. For God to give us a full measure of regeneration and sanctification in an instant would be like parents bringing their newborn home from the hospital and presenting her with a stroller, tricycle, scooter, bicycle, and car all at the same time.

4. *Sanctification begins when God forgives us of our sins and gives us new birth, and it grows incrementally throughout the rest of our lives on earth.*

This interpretation sees sanctification impacted in a believer's life progressively over the long haul of living. As a believer reads the Bible, prays, attends church services, and turns to the other channels of God's grace, he or she becomes more aware of the sinful nature still residing deep within the heart. Being grieved by this sinful nature, the believer enters conflict between flesh and spirit. He or she prays constantly, asking God to grant victory in this daily battle to live rightly and avoid evil. This results in a constant uphill struggle.

This interpretation holds that the struggle against sin continues as long as we live in a human body, because much of our trouble comes from the body. Those who hold this interpretation say with Walt Whitman, "It was not I that sinned the sin, / The ruthless body dragged me in. / Though long I strove courageously, / The body was too much for me."[2]

However, slowly but surely over time, the spiritual nature wins more battles than the fleshly nature. Sanctification becomes the dominant influence in the believer's life. This struggle and growth process continues until death.

This interpretation makes a lot of sense logically and biblically. Objections to the other interpretations find answers in this one. It approaches growth according to the level of our understanding rather than giving us the entire spiritual package in one deposit. It provides us with the benefits of sanctification in the daily grind of life rather than at the point of death or after death's visit.

Lurking problems with this interpretation, unfortunately, leave it inadequate. It straps us in a lifelong struggle against the sinful nature. Spiritual growth appears to be more a matter of trained growth or developing new habits than of appropriating the gift of God's grace. It emphasizes my striving and exercising willpower rather than God's miraculous work of character transformation.

> **Spiritual growth appears to be more a matter of trained growth or developing new habits than of appropriating the gift of God's grace.**

Worst of all, it calls for us to grow out of selfishness or self-centeredness. Our problem with self goes far deeper than our ability to simply tame it like a house pet. A series of spiritually wise choices, even over a long period of time, cannot cure self-centeredness. Only God's cleansing work can adequately deal with the culprit.

5. *Sanctification begins in the new birth, grows with spiritual development to the time of a second moment when the Spirit takes complete control, then develops incrementally in maturity throughout a believer's life.*

The explanation of this interpretation sounds more complicated than it is. The ETA of this view occurs at several intersection points in the believer's life. Each of these intersection points goes by a different label.

First, God begins His transforming work in us the moment He forgives us of our past sins and gives us new birth. The minute we become new creatures in Christ, we begin to exhibit a changed life. Old patterns of sinful living give way to new patterns of righteous living. Because it occurs at the very beginning of the Christian walk, we call this *initial sanctification.*

Spiritual and personal growth occur each time we make a godly decision or resist a temptation. Moral muscle develops. We progressively establish habits of righteous living. We also begin to mature in our faith as we look and act like a follower of Jesus Christ. Thus, we call this stage *progressive sanctification*.

At some point along the Christian journey, we rendezvous with a moment when we must come to terms more decisively than ever before with Christ's claims of Lordship on us. In loving response, we·offer ourselves as a living sacrifice for God and His service (Rom. 12:1-2). God accepts our consecration and sanctifies every part of our being (1 Thess. 5:23-24). The language of this last scripture passage leads us to call this moment *entire sanctification*.

> *Sanctification speaks of a connection with divinity not trip No. 2 to the front of the church.*

Following entire sanctification, we believers experience more progressive growth in maturity through the rest of our earthly walks. None of these facets of sanctification constitute a static experience that we name, claim, and place in the trophy case of spiritual accomplishments. They do not give us the satisfaction of another notch on our belt of spiritual experience.

In fact, even talking about sanctification in terms of a static experience misses the entire vitality of its reality. These various intersection points with God far exceed the language of an experience. They are not religious mountains to be simply conquered and recorded. They represent flawed attempts of language to capture in words common encounters that believers have with God in the expanding nature of their relationship. Thus, sanctification speaks of a connection with divinity not trip No. 2 to the front of the church.

This last interpretation has its limitations just as the others do. However, it attempts to incorporate the many biblical references to sanctification and holiness into its scope. It also tries to make sense of believers' various experiences with God.

A Requirement for Salvation?

People frequently ask me, "Do I have to have a second spiritual experience of sanctification to get into heaven?"

My answer depends on several factors, such as the age, spiritual maturity level, and growth rate of the believer. I'll answer no if you simply mean a second spiritual experience. Our salvation becomes a reality the minute we accept Jesus Christ as Savior."

Those who answer an unquestionable yes to that notion misinterpret Heb. 12:14, "Without holiness no one will see the Lord." In this passage holiness refers generally to the righteous life of a godly person, not a second spiritual experience.

Shortly after giving this response in a Christian magazine article, I received a strong letter from a reader who told me about his relative who accepted Christ one day, asked for sanctification the next day, and died on the third day. He wrote, "I firmly believe if my relative had not asked for sanctification that second day, he would have gone to hell."

I couldn't disagree more. Our salvation centers in trusting Christ as Savior, not logging spiritual experiences.

Now, if the Holy Spirit impresses on a believer's heart the need for a deeper commitment, and that person turns his or her back on God, the relationship can be threatened. We cannot continue our walk with God and willfully walk behind the light of His direction for our lives. We must go where He leads.

A Practical Analysis

Our sanctification discussion leads to the following practical analysis. Through progressive growth in God's grace, I reach a point in my spiritual journey at which I realize I face a spiritual struggle. I need God to do something more in my heart. It's not that my spiritual fire has died. Rather, God's presence creates a hunger for a deeper relationship with Him.

Until God creates that hunger, I'm not likely to seek a deeper work. But, once I realize my need for more of God's grace, I offer or consecrate myself to Him. I make my offer with faith that He will accept it. He does accept this offer, not over the long haul of life, but in a moment of time, the same way a friend offers me a gift, and I accept it.

> *Some compare the cleansing of our sinful nature with images of pulling a decayed tooth or blowing a tree stump out of the ground.*

This new level of commitment on my part gives God greater latitude to work His miracle of grace in me. My self-preference dies in a moment, in its place—God-preference. My self-centeredness bows to Christ-centeredness. More than anything else in life, I want what God wants for me. However, just as a child learns to talk and walk, read and write slowly over a long period of time, so to, my life becomes more Christlike, more conformed to the image of God in small, incremental steps. Growth continues for as long as I serve Him.

Because sanctification focuses more on relationship with God than on a static experience, I must continue to walk daily in God's light. Metaphors from days gone by have created unrealistic understandings of what actually happens. Some compare the cleansing of our sinful nature with images of pulling a decayed tooth or blowing a tree stump out of the ground. Once a bad tooth or a stump has been removed, it cannot come back.

However, since the sinful nature is more a way of valuing and prioritizing my preferences, I can revert to a sinful way of preferring myself anytime I want. That's why the metaphor of an infection better captures the concept. God can heal the infection of my nature, but I can become reinfected if I don't let Him continually cleanse me. God's work of sanctification in me is decisive but is also conditional on my openness to His constant cleansing grace. That's why our relationship with God is so vital. We must do as Norman Vincent Peale urges, "Ask God who made you to keep on remaking you."[3]

A Biblical Approach

Each element of this last interpretation attempts to appropriate biblical directives concerning our sanctification. Here are just a few of the central features incorporated into this interpretation.

1. A baptism as an event in time—"He will baptize you with the Holy Spirit and with fire" (Matt. 3:11).

2. A seal as the Holy Spirit impresses His signet ring on the warm wax of our soul in a moment. "And you also were included in Christ when you heard the word of truth, the gospel of your salvation. Having believed, you were marked in him with a seal, the promised Holy Spirit" (Eph. 1:13). See also 2 Cor. 1:22 below.

3. A down payment placed on a piece of property, promising full payment to come. "Set his seal of ownership on us, and put his Spirit in our hearts as a deposit, guaranteeing what is to come" (2 Cor. 1:22).

4. A circumcision of the heart that happens in a moment. "Circumcision is circumcision of the heart, by the Spirit, not by the written code" (Rom. 2:29). See also Col. 2:9-15.

5. A crucifixion of the old sinful nature as a decisive event in time. "For we know that our old self was crucified with him so that the body of sin might be done away with, that we should no longer be slaves to sin" (Rom. 6:6). See also Gal. 2:20, "I have been crucified with Christ and I no longer live, but Christ lives in me. The life I live in the body, I live by faith in the Son of God, who loved me and gave himself for me."

6. A cleansing act. "Husbands, love your wives, just as Christ loved

the church and gave himself up for her to make her holy, cleansing her by the washing with water through the word, and to present her to himself as a radiant church, without stain or wrinkle or any other blemish, but holy and blameless" (Eph. 5:25-27).

7. A clothing with spiritual power as an event. "I am going to send you what my Father has promised; but stay in the city until you have been clothed with power from on high" (Luke 24:49).

8. An invitation to live under the full direction of the Helper (John 13—17).

9. A death to sin for full life in God. "In the same way, count yourselves dead to sin but alive to God in Christ Jesus" (Rom. 6:11).

10. A consecration of self to God. "Therefore, I urge you, brothers, in view of God's mercy, to offer your bodies as living sacrifices, holy and pleasing to God—this is your spiritual act of worship. Do not conform any longer to the pattern of this world, but be transformed by the renewing of your mind. Then you will be able to test and approve what God's will is—his good, pleasing and perfect will" (Rom. 12:1-2).

11. A temple of the Holy Spirit. "Don't you know that you yourselves are God's temple and that God's Spirit lives in you? . . . for God's temple is sacred, and you are that temple (1 Cor. 3:16-17). See also 1 Cor. 6:19-20.

12. A purification. "Since we have these promises, dear friends, let us purify ourselves from everything that contaminates body and spirit, perfecting holiness out of reverence for God" (2 Cor. 7:1).

13. Taking off dirty clothes and putting on clean ones. "Put off your old self, which is being corrupted by its deceitful desires; to be made new in the attitude of your minds; and to put on the new self, created to be like God in true righteousness and holiness" (Eph. 4:22-24).

14. A renewable Spirit filling. "Be filled with the Spirit" (Eph. 5:18).

15. A work of completion. "May God himself, the God of peace, sanctify you through and through. May your whole spirit, soul and body be kept blameless at the coming of our Lord Jesus Christ. The one who calls you is faithful and he will do it" (1 Thess. 5:23-24).

16. The acceptance of a call. "But just as he who called you is holy, so be holy in all you do; for it is written: 'Be holy, because I am holy'" (1 Pet. 1:15-16).

A Love Affair

My love affair with my wife, Sue, best illustrates our spiritual journey. Did my love for her happen in a moment of time or has it happened over the past 27 years? Yes!

After dating Sue for several weeks, I realized I loved her more than any other girl on our college campus. At a moment in time on a Thursday evening, I sat in my car in front of my college dormitory and acknowledged that fact. I quickly ran to a phone, called her, and told her how I felt. At another moment in time, I proposed marriage to her. At still another moment, I stood in front of a church filled with people and pledged my commitment to her for a lifetime.

> *Every day for the past 27 years my love for Sue has quietly deepened.*

It is important to remember that while love connected us, we did not simply start living together once we recognized love's presence. We sealed our commitment in a consecrating moment before God and a church filled with witnesses. Then we ate cake and drank punch together. In one moment we were engaged; following the wedding ceremony, husband and wife.

That moment was incredibly important to the relationship. However, our love did not only grow when I first told her I loved her, when I asked her to marry me, and when we married. We did not enter a static experience at the altar recorded only in glossy photos. Every day for the past 27 years my love for Sue has quietly deepened. It will continue to develop and mature as long as we live together and love each other. Because our love is a relationship, we must nurture it and one another daily.

This analogy works well because our faith in God is also a love relationship marked by critical moments of decision and lots of slow growth over time. Marriage far exceeds the language of an experience or a noble social ideal. It encompasses a living, breathing relationship with another eternal soul. It points to a mystery defying description. Just as marriage is so much more than a couple of points in time, we cannot capture our relationship with God in weak words.

God sanctifies us in a moment in time and conforms us to the image of His Son over the course of a lifetime. The ETA all depends on our level of spiritual development and openness to His desire to work more fully in us. If we are willing, He can accomplish His good plans in us.

Fast Takes

1. Sanctification is far too complex a relationship with God to reduce to a few simple formulas.

2. While believers agree the Bible teaches sanctification, they often disagree on the interpretation of scriptural references.

3. Sanctification involves both moments in time when God deals decisively with us spiritually and long periods of slow growth.

4. God works with us according to the level of our understanding and draws us closer to Him as we realize our need for a deeper work of grace.

5. Our relationship with God in sanctification parallels our love life with our mate in many ways.

Think About This . . .

1. How do our different backgrounds, personalities, and interpretations of Scripture affect the way we see sanctification?

2. What do you like most about the idea of getting sanctification after you die? What do you like least about it?

3. What do you like most about the idea of getting sanctification just before you die? What do you like least about it?

4. What do you like most about the idea of getting sanctification at the time of new birth? What do you like least about it?

5. What do you like most about the idea of getting sanctification incrementally throughout life? What do you like least about it?

6. What value do you see in the last interpretation offered for the ETA of sanctification? What are the drawbacks of this view?

7. Gives examples or testimony of how God works His miracle of sanctification in a moment of time.

8. Give examples or testimony of how sanctification is a growing process.

9. Look over the 16 biblical concepts of sanctification. Have most or all of them been incorporated into the last interpretation offered for the ETA of sanctification?

10. Add your own ideas to the way sanctification is like a love affair.

In this is perfection, and glory and happiness:
the royal law of heaven and earth is this,
"Thou shalt love the Lord thy God with all thy heart,
and with all thy soul, and with all thy mind,
and with all thy strength." The one perfect
good shall be your ultimate end.

—*John Wesley*[1]

9

PERFECT YET?

A Nightmare Come True

Sue and I were on another of our spring break trips with 25 university students in a third world setting for compassionate ministry. We built a school, distributed health supplies, and witnessed for Christ in various ways. Sue became quite ill during the week, running a high fever with body aches and coughing.

What a nightmare! She was so sick, in fact, I doubted if she could make the 24-hour trip home. A Christian doctor gave her some medicine that made her sleep on the plane, and we anxiously started for the United States. The trip was hard on Sue's body.

When we arrived home and visited our physician, he scheduled immediate surgery to locate the source of her mysterious illness. In the operating room the surgeon discovered something he had never seen before. He did not know how to diagnosis her condition. Something had destroyed one of her lymph glands, so he removed it.

We later learned her illness resulted from a rare infectious disease. It took her a year to fully recover from its effects. Later tests revealed permanent scarring on her lungs. To this day, whenever Sue gets a chest X ray, those scars appear. She enjoys good health now but will carry the scars of that illness as long as she lives.

Remaining Scars

Consecrating ourselves to God opens the way to His gift of entire sanctification. God heals the infection inflicted on us by Adam and Eve's poor choice. He restores our heart to the way He intended us to be in His original plan. A soul restored to health, however, does not erase history—like erasing a computer disk—and return us to the innocence we enjoyed before the forbidden fruit feast. We still live in a world stained by the effects of sinful choices made both today and down through the ages.

We also still live with the memory of our own past rebellion against God and our mistakes. We are all too aware of our inadequacies. God heals the infection, but scars remain.

> *A soul restored to health does not erase history and return us to the innocence enjoyed prior to the forbidden fruit feast.*

More than a Lab Frog

God's sanctifying work changes our spiritual nature. We expect an encounter with God to affect us spiritually. However, remember those famous words of the television advertiser, "But wait. There's more!" Not only does God work with our spirit, but He works with all other areas of our lives as well.

Because of the complexities of humanity, it's difficult to fully examine all aspects of our nature. To get to the real human heart, you cannot dissect it and put pushpins with paper labels on various parts of it like we did in 10th grade biology class with our smelly laboratory frogs. Besides their spiritual natures, people have:

1. An intellect with imagination, memory, and reasoning ability
2. A full range of emotions and a whole set of physical and psychological factors that effect those emotions
3. A conscience that serves as a moral compass or global positioning system as in airplanes and expensive cars
4. A free will that chooses courses of action and reaction to various life experiences
5. A sense of humor with a set of criteria as to what makes something funny
6. An entire set of social skills and guidelines for living in society with other people
7. A whole range of personal likes and dislikes that create unique individuals

Into this complex individual, God's Spirit comes to control and direct. This control does not happen automatically as when you install a new program on your computer that automatically updates all of your files. God's Spirit works in each of these areas according to the degree to which we become aware of His Lordship in that particular area and consciously invite Him to instruct us. One by one the arenas of a person's life receive the influence of God's Spirit to provide anything lacking. This leads to wholeness and health just as our spirit received health with the healing of "The Infection."

Rough Edges

This speaks to a very important question often asked in holiness circles. For instance, "If God has sanctified Allen, why does he still have so many rough edges?"

Because entire sanctification begins in a moment of time, but the meticulous process of applying it to every aspect of our lives takes a lifetime.

Let me illustrate. We installed a new electronic card catalog system in our university library three years ago. Each of 90,000 books had to be individually entered into the system. It took hundreds of hours of work. Likewise, once we offer God's Spirit full control of the center of our being, He works over the course of a lifetime impacting and changing us, little by little. As Orel Hershiser put it, "Christianity is called a spiritual walk. It's not a run and it's not a jog. It's a walk you do from day to day."[2]

The damage sustained in the Fall affected more than just our spiritual nature. It stained bone deep. It infected every other part of our being, thus affecting the way we understand and relate to ourselves and those with whom we live and work.

God works with us over time, in keeping with our level of understanding, to smooth off our rough edges and give us a better understanding of ourselves and our place in the world. He helps us change the things about ourselves we need to change, and He helps us accept those areas of our lives that will remain blemished. He also helps us in our relationships with ourselves and others.

Goals Toward Which We Strive

God moves us in the direction of maturity throughout our lives and works in various ways in the following areas of life. To each of these areas the Holy Spirit offers direction and helps us in necessary improvements. It's a long list, so read it slowly and think how each item measures up in your life.

1. Loving God and others with our entire being
2. Using free will to choose God's ways and avoid evil choices and attitudes
3. Relating well to others, tolerant of social and personal differences
4. Preferring the needs of others over our own needs
5. Showing compassion to needy people

6. Emotional stability

7. Coping skills to adjust to the difficulties and changing circumstances of life

8. Accepting our sexuality and practicing proper expression within biblical guidelines

9. Proper management of money and material possessions

10. Proper understanding of risks, danger, and death

11. Effective management of time

12. Proper balance between work and play, responsibility and recreation

13. Proper understanding of our skills and abilities

14. Ability to live with ambiguity and unanswered questions in life

15. Growing discernment of and sensitivity to evil and the subtle ways it tempts believers

16. Ability to discern between essentials and nonessentials

17. Sacrificing the good for the best

18. Establishing priorities from wishful desires

19. Training our conscience and remaining sensitive to it

20. Being aware of our appetites, passions, and drives in order to control them properly

21. Being aware of our weaknesses, prejudices, and negative tendencies in order to develop or correct them

22. Understanding our normal mood swings, learning to control the highs and lows of the cycle so as not to create stress on family and friends

23. Willfully accepting persecution for the cause of Christ

24. Properly understanding our place in the world

25. Properly understanding the purpose of life and being governed by a personal life philosophy

Means of Grace

That's a lifetime homework assignment, right? How does God teach us these life lessons? Through a variety of ways we call means of grace. These means of grace exemplify ways God graces us with His instruction. Here is a partial list of the methods God uses.

Prayer involves two-way communion with God. Its purpose is to bring us in alignment with God's will, not to get God to do our bidding. As Phillips Brooks put it, "Prayer is not conquering God's reluctance but taking hold of God's willingness."[3] We pray throughout the day both for our own needs and the needs of others. Many appointments fill our date books, but we must never become too busy to pray.

Meditation involves sitting and listening quietly for God's whispering voice. We prefer lights and action, such as when God appeared to the Hebrew nation at Mount Sinai. Now that was a fireworks show! I wish God always revealed His will in fireworks or banners pulled behind airplanes. Unfortunately, He seldom manifests himself in such ways. More often than not, it's in a gentle whisper and a soft nudge. We have to slow down and get still enough to hear Him.

We also must make time to *read Scripture*. We need to read a translation we understand and use Bible study helps. When we determine the meaning of a particular passage, we must then apply it to our lives. The Bible addresses every area of life and offers helpful directives on how to deal with particular situations.

We must *attend church regularly* and *worship God* with fellow believers. Corporate worship offers us an opportunity to contemplate God together. Singing and corporate prayer further aid our worship experience. The centerpiece of corporate worship is the message from God's Word presented by God's spokesperson.

Beyond corporate worship, believers need time to *fellowship* together. We need to talk, laugh, cry, and play with one another. Jesus met often with small groups of friends in various locations. We should do the same. In the process, God teaches us about our personal walk with Him as we learn how He leads our friends.

At times on the journey of faith, we feel more compelled to pray than eat. At those times we deny our physical hungers and invest the energy in our prayer concerns. These times of *fasting* not only draw us close to God but also bring physical benefits. Fasting may not be a required discipline, but God uses it in beneficial ways.

Horses have bridles; dogs have leashes; we have *discipline*. We must learn to control every area of our lives. As Epictetus put it, "No man is free who is not master of himself."[4] We must control our eating habits and weight. We must exercise our bodies and care for them. We must control our speech to avoid unwholesome language, questionable humor, complaining, and gossip. We must control our moods and feelings. And we must control our spending habits to avoid the idol of materialism.

God also speaks to us through *selfless service*. We speak often of giving our time and money to the local church; that's good. However, we must also give time and energy to serving the needs of others outside the church. Helen Keller rightly said, "Life is an exciting business and most exciting when it is lived for others."[5]

It's so natural for us to think only of our own needs and those of our family and friends. It's tempting to become ingrown. God's grace instructs us to give our lives away for the sake of others. God provides opportunity for great growth here, but as Thomas Edison reminded, "Opportunity is missed by most people because it is dressed in overalls and looks like work."[6]

We do not often speak of it, but God also teaches us valuable lessons when we go through dark valleys of *suffering*. Suffering can help us grow in character. It teaches us lessons of obedience when dark clouds hang low. It also reminds us of how much Christ suffered and that sometimes suffering is necessary for a greater good to emerge.

Paul reminds us, "Now I rejoice in what was suffered for you, and I fill up in my flesh what is still lacking in regard to Christ's afflictions, for the sake of his body, which is the church" (Col. 1:24). This does not mean Christ did not completely pay the price for our salvation on the Cross. It means if we live and witness for Christ, we will suffer for His cause.

Many oppose the gospel message; Satan establishes roadblocks to our Christian service. Being involved in Christ's work includes accepting the suffering that goes with it. Whether that suffering involves being ridiculed at school, having our property damaged, or being persecuted to death, Christ's followers step forward to pay the price. In that suffering, God teaches us many valuable spiritual lessons. We must do as Thomas à Kempis reminded, "Carry the cross patiently, and with perfect submission; and in the end it shall carry you."[7]

Growth Points

Though the picture may never be fully complete in this life, God hopes for growth in the intricate parts of our complex being. We should:

1. Have a habit of living daily in dependence upon the Holy Spirit
2. Bring our appetites, instincts, and aspirations to God for His direction in their proper fulfillment
3. Love and accept ourselves properly
4. Love our neighbor as we love ourselves
5. Have right desires and turn them into conduct
6. Increasingly conform to God's will
7. Properly balance between no rules and too many rules, no possessions and materialism, ignoring others' needs and spending ourselves into emotional and financial bankruptcy
8. Regularly give ourselves in service to others[8]

In all of these ways, God instructs and develops us. However, when He dismisses "class" each day, He depends on us to put feet to the truths He has taught us, and to bring them to reality. As Mother Teresa said, "My progress in holiness depends on God and myself: on God's grace and my will."[9]

Here's a great reminder from Otho Jennings, former professor at Asbury College:

God answers prayer, but we must do the praying. God's grace provides the ground for faith, but man must do the believing. God puts His love in our hearts, but He will never love our neighbor for us; we must do the loving. God gives us strength to resist temptation, but we must will to resist. God provides food for our souls, but we must do the eating. God has planned for us a life of growth in grace, but we must do the growing. In short, God through the death of His Son upon the Cross has made ample provision that we should be holy; but the acceptance by free will of these provisions is the sole responsibility of man.[10]

> *When He dismisses class each day, He depends on us to put feet to the truths He has taught us and to make them a reality in our lives.*

Perfect Yet?

Folks frequently ask, "Does sanctification make me perfect as Jesus calls us in Matt. 5:48, 'Be perfect, therefore, as your heavenly Father is perfect'?"

That depends on how you define *perfect*. If you're talking about perfect performance, the answer is no. Maturity and growth bring that over long periods of time. A touch of God's hand does not make me more cultured or refined, so that I eat my soup properly and enjoy visiting an art museum.

If you're talking about perfect motive or desire to please God, the answer is yes. More than anything else in the world, my new openness to God increases my desire to please Him.

So what about this call to be perfect in light of the difference between perfect performance and perfect desire? Let me address that question with this illustration.

I took Brent with me one day to get gas in our van. He was about 10 years old at the time. When I got out of the van to pump the gas, he got out and started cleaning the windshield. He wasn't tall enough to reach the top of the windshield with the cleaning brush nor strong enough to press hard. We'd driven home the night before through some pretty dense bug populations. Dozens of bugs had gone to eternity from our windshield.

When I finished pumping the gas and got back in the van, I couldn't believe the two sights that faced me. One was a son with a smile stretched from ear to ear saying, "Look, Dad. I cleaned the windshield for you. I love you, Dad." The other sight was a windshield with bugs smeared so badly I could hardly see to drive. It looked like he'd smeared raw scrambled eggs all over it.

Was Brent perfect? You tell me. What do you think I saw: a flawed performance or a willing heart? I thanked him for his thoughtfulness and silently prayed I wouldn't kill us both on the drive home! Brent's attempt was perfect as far as this dad measured it. And you can rest assured our Heavenly Father feels the same way about our efforts at holy living. Is the performance always flawless? No. Can the desire of our hearts be pure and clean? You bet.

So, give yourself completely to the Father. Let Him purify your heart by faith and fill you completely with His Spirit. Hold nothing back. Live every day in the light of His instruction and grow in Him.

Fast Takes

1. Even though God restores our heart to good health in sanctification, He cannot return us to our perfect condition prior to the Fall.

2. People are complex beings with many parts that interact and affect the way we live and respond.

3. The Spirit's influence on each of our complex parts is not automatic. He works over time, to the degree to which we invite His instruction and direction.

4. God instructs us through His means of grace: prayer, meditation, Scripture reading, corporate worship, Christian fellowship, fasting, self-discipline, selfless service, and suffering.

5. Though we may never perform perfectly in every area of life, we can have a pure heart and desire to please God and serve others.

Think About This . . .

1. What scars from your past will remain in your life for the rest of the journey?

2. How do the various parts of your being described in "More than a Lab Frog" relate to each other in your life?

3. In the 25 "Goals Toward Which We Strive," which are your best strengths?

4. Which goals need more attention in your life?

5. Why does God require us to work for improvements in our lives? Why doesn't He make the improvements automatic and take the work out of it?

6. Think again about the difference between perfect performance and perfect desire. Summarize in your own words what God expects of you.

Advertising is the only kind of news
found in the daily papers that's
always on the bright side.[1]

FALSE ADVERTISING

Hard Lesson

I watched out our living room window for the mailman's truck every morning that eighth summer of my life. As soon as he completed his delivery to our rural mailbox, I ran down the lane to see if the postman delivered my package. The advertisement on the back of the cereal box said my order would arrive in about two weeks. Exactly 14 days passed, and my patience had expired. I had saved box tops from cereal boxes for several months.

Finally, I had enough tops to claim my prize—a toy gun. The advertisement called it a limited edition, silver-plated item to cherish for years to come. I could hardly believe my good fortune to claim such a special possession for only a few cereal box tops and $2 postage. But the ad said I'd get in on the limited offer if I responded quickly. "If it's in print, it must be true," I thought.

Day after day my anticipations collapsed as the mailbox handed me more junk mail. I scuffed my tennis shoes through the gravel and moped back to the house. Two weeks came and went, then three. Finally about four weeks after I placed the order, a paper-mailing envelope arrived with my name on it. I had no idea what might be in it. It surely wasn't my limited-edition, silver-plated, to-cherish-for-years-to-come gun! The manufacturer would never put such a valued item in such a cheap envelope.

I tore the envelope open and couldn't believe my eyes. Into my hand fell a small, cheap, plastic toy gun. The barrel had inferior silver paint sprayed onto it. The trigger hardly worked. A worthless piece of junk!

False Claims

I learned an important lesson that day about advertisements. You don't always get what you bargain for. Advertising claims bombard us daily. They come from every direction. Radio, television, newspapers, magazines, and billboards all cry for our attention—and our money.

No amount of faith and no religious experience will change us into either heavenly beings or creatures possessing divinity in this life or the next.

Some advertising claims ring true; most of them bloat with hype. Advertisements often weigh in strong with promises but prove to be rather weak when the light of truth shines on them. That's OK. We've grown so accustomed to their exaggeration that we discount most of their claims anyway. We know to write them off as false advertising.

Unfortunately, false advertising has sometimes invaded the church with claims of what holiness accomplishes in believers. I've heard that holiness will end your mood swings, solve all of your personal relationship problems, keep you on a perpetual spiritual high, give you colorful visions of God, take away all of your dysfunctional family struggles, create celestial images with bright lights and heavenly music. But, worst of all, I have heard that holiness will end temptation's power and all possibility for sinning.

The Claims

God does many wonderful things in our lives through our consecration and His sanctification. However, He doesn't do some of the things people claim. Consider the following advertising claims I've heard.

1. *"Holiness makes me like God's angels."*

These folks have been watching too many angel programs on television. Holiness does not make us angelic or divine. We sometimes call our children "little angels," but that doesn't transform them into heavenly beings. Some false religions teach that if you follow their teachings, you will become divine when you die. Great claim! No proof that they can deliver on their promise; no money-back guarantee with this one!

No amount of faith and no religious experience will change us into either heavenly beings or creatures possessing divinity in this life or the next. We're still full-fledged citizens of the human race with our feet planted firmly on earth's soil.

2. *"I live in constant communion with God throughout every day."*

Oh, please! The apostle Paul didn't even claim that. Holiness does not give us uninterrupted contact with God. Some people put me to shame and give me an inferiority complex about my spirituality. The way they tell it, they have a high-speed Internet connection to God with constant updates coming from the heavenly throne. It sounds great; but it's just not true. As a sanctified believer, you will still experience dry seasons and times when heaven seems off the radar screen.

The Internet server goes down at my university at times. When it happens, I get a message on my computer screen that I'm "off-line" for the time being. That puts me out of touch with the worldwide web. An infinite combination of reasons can create the same feeling about our accessibility to God. Even though He's as near as our quietest whisper, we don't feel Him. Total commitment to God does not keep us from feeling disconnected at times. That's where blind trust and faith in Him step up to the plate.

> *You will still experience dry seasons and times when heaven seems off the radar screen.*

3. *"The minute God sanctified me, I became outgoing and confident enough to talk to anyone."*

Holiness does not immediately change your personality type. I wish it did. We could all solve our personality problems in a moment. I have heard people tell how their commitment to God revolutionized their personality to the point that they hardly believed the different person they instantly became. Nevertheless, it doesn't happen that way for most of us. An extrovert will still have plenty to say to the stranger in the grocery store checkout line. An introvert will still tend to hide in the shadows at the back of the room.

Granted, daily fellowship with God helps us become more polished in social settings, but it does not automatically alter who we have been for decades. Sanctified believers still need to look in the mirror and adjust their behavior when necessary. These adjustments take effort, not simply a divine touch.

4. *"I used to have mood swings, but not since I got sanctified. No more highs and lows for me, thank God!"*

What kind of pills are these people taking? Holiness does not change your basic temperament. Each of us has our own characteristic or usual emotional responses in particular situations. This usual response is as unique to each of us as our fingerprints. Some people are naturally nervous and easily excitable; others are sensitive and easily disturbed. Each of us has our own pattern of mood swings that mark our individuality.

Some look on the dark side of every situation and have a tendency toward negative thoughts. Some see the glass half full rather than half empty. God deals with these issues one by one, and we work on them. But we don't suddenly begin to act in unusual new ways.

All of the mental characteristics that belong to each of us and determine our basic temperament create our identity. While we certainly must master these characteristics so we do not live or respond in ways that betray Christ, we must also realize our relationship with God does not automatically or instantly change these characteristics. We developed them over time, and we will change them over time.

5. *"Since I gave everything to God, I don't get discouraged."*

I hear this sometimes from my 20-something friends. This creates a real problem since their peers tend to be discouraged. When discouragement knocks at their door, they refuse to answer it. But the uninvited guest finds a way through the back door anyway. This lofty claim beats the average young believer into the ground. It is unrealistic because discouragement has such a nebulous origin. It's seldom a matter of spiritual weakness.

Some people respond to discouragement by feeling a bit sad; others become dissatisfied with a situation in life. It can result from a physical or mental illness, from disappointment over bad news or a personal failure, from a financial reversal or a negative turn of events at work. In none of these cases does our walk with God prevent us from feeling the normal human reaction of discouragement.

Our normal patterns of response or reaction do not transform into different patterns immediately upon our decision to give ourselves more fully to God.

To say that saints never get discouraged forces conscientious followers of Christ to hide their natural responses to life's downturns. Some of the most godly saints in the Bible and church history experienced discouragement, some severe depression. We may become discouraged too.

6. *"Nothing ever frustrates or stresses me since the Holy Spirit took control."*

Holiness does not instantly change the way we react when frustrated or provoked. Over time we develop patterns of responding to the positive and negative things that happen. We become so predictable that those who live with us and know us best can forecast how we will respond in a particular situation. That's why we find it so amusing to play practical jokes on our friends—because we enjoy doing things that we know will provoke their response. We take pleasure in watching them react predictably.

Our normal patterns of response or reaction do not transform immediately when we decide to give ourselves more fully to God. That is because these patterns are not spiritual or unspiritual in themselves. Since they are learned reactions, some may need to be redirected. That requires our effort, not a mere dramatic touch from God.

7. *"God has taken all human hungers away from me. It's as if I never had them."*

Come on. Get real! You don't lose human hungers in a religious experience; you lose them from brainwashing or disconnecting your mind from your human nature. Holiness does not take away normal human hungers for things like food, sex, success, recreation, and appreciation. God created us with these human hungers for a reason.

If we did not have hunger pains, we might forget to eat (I probably wouldn't, but some might). Malnutrition would eventually lead to death. If we did not have a hunger for sexual expression, we might not get around to finding a mate, getting married, and starting a family. If too many people failed in this way, the human race would become extinct. (Don't expect an epidemic of this hunger loss anytime soon!)

God programmed us with an urge to do our best and accomplish things with our lives. These accomplishments benchmark successes along life's road. Something inside of us strives for significant achievements. However, we cannot labor for success all of the time. We must balance our days, weeks, and years with times of recreation. We step away from our task to play or rest for a while. Times of recreation are in God's cycle as well.

When we do a good job or attempt good deeds for others, it's natural to want others to acknowledge our efforts with words of appreciation. All of these things—food, sex, success, recreation, and appreciation—are neither spiritual nor carnal themselves. But the way we satisfy them can be good or bad. We must learn to control these hungers and express them according to God's plan for our lives.

8. *"I used to struggle with my nerves, but one trip to the altar solved that problem."*

Nerves run through our bodies just as muscles, bones, and blood vessels do. They carry pleasure and pain signals throughout our frame. We're all wired a little differently. I flinch at sudden noises; Sue remains steady if a firecracker goes off behind her head.

We're exposed to annoyances throughout the day. Noisy neighbors, barking dogs, buzzing house flies, crying children. Regardless of the source,

> **No amount of religion will keep a chirping cricket in your bedroom at night from getting on your nerves.**

such disturbances finally get the best of us; some of us react sooner or different from others.

Does faith in God mean life's irritations won't get under my skin? Never! No amount of religion will keep a chirping cricket in your bedroom at night from getting on your nerves. Holiness does not solve all nerve problems, either. One person's nerves may be just as weak as another person's back.

I'll never forget my godly grandmother's response when she had been locked up with my sister, two brothers, and me for too long a period of time: "You children are really getting on Grandma's nerves." That meant, "Get lost before Grandma blows a gasket."

I remember a time during our first pastorate when Sue, one of our faithful church members, came to the altar to pray for a special work of God in her life. After listening to her describe her typical day, I advised, "Quit praying; go home, take a hot bath, and go to bed."

She didn't need more religion; she needed to give her nerves a break from the household responsibilities a husband and six children bring into a woman's life. Several days of rest with the kids out of the house put her back on top spiritually. We must watch out for the little irritations of life, for as Benjamin Franklin said, "Watch the little things; a small leak will sink a great ship."[2]

9. *"Since God sanctified me, I have become immune to temptation.*

This is a common misunderstanding about holiness. I hear it referred to in one way or another rather frequently. It flows from an incorrect use of logic. The line of logic goes something like this: I have given God every part of my being and have turned from selfish ways. His will fully works in me. The Holy Spirit fills me. Therefore, I cannot be tempted to sin. My closeness to God lifts me out of temptation's reach.

As long as I live, I will never forget the words of a sobbing married woman who visited my office the morning after she'd experienced a terrible moral failure. After explaining how she and a married man from our church ended up at a cheap motel, she said, "But, I thought once I was sanctified, it was no longer possible for me to sin. I wasn't even guarding myself because I didn't think I could fall."

She thought her sanctification vaccinated her from the possibility of making wrong choices. Unfortunately, she believed a false claim made by some of her Christian friends.

Holiness does not end the possibility for temptation or sin. Study the Scriptures. All the saints of the Bible resisted temptations. Temptation even knocked at Jesus' door, the closest man to the Father who ever lived on this earth. As long as we live on this side of eternity, Satan will suggest ways to satisfy legitimate desires wrongly or derail God's plan. We must say no daily.

10. *"Holiness took care of all my relationship problems with people."*

Like the saying goes, "Birds of a feather flock together." We tend to gravitate toward people who think and act like we do. We understand them and enjoy spending time with them. But not everyone thinks and acts the way I do. For some reason, certain people like coffee, asparagus, staying up late, putting assignments off until the last minute, loud music, and playing in the snow. I don't. I prefer hot chocolate, fried okra, going to bed at 10 P.M., planning ahead, contemporary Christian music, and the beach.

I don't always understand why people think the way they think or act the way they act. Some of their preferences are just plain weird, as I see it. And then again, part of our irritation with one another might be like the old Pennsylvania Dutch proverb says, "Our faults irritate us most when we see them in others."[3]

> *Thank the Lord, I don't have any idiosyncrasies!*

Since we're all so different or irritate one another, we sometimes have relationship problems. Holiness does not fix all of those problems. Sanctified believers must work at relationships just like everyone else. We must be loving toward one another, prefer others whenever possible, be courteous toward others' opinions or ways of doing things, and be patient with their idiosyncrasies.

Thank the Lord, I don't have any idiosyncrasies; just ask my wife. On second thought, don't ask her. Remember, living harmoniously with others is a developed art, not a spiritual gift. As David Grayson reminds, "Commandment Number One of any truly civilized society is this: Let people be different."[4]

11. *"Holiness solved all of my expressions of anger. Nothing bothers me anymore."*

This false claim is more complicated than some of the other claims, because anger, like many emotions, springs from different sources. Some sources are consistent with the Christian walk, others are not.

An unholy anger often manifests itself as vindictive passion rising suddenly and resulting in emotional outbursts or actions. It may result from hitting your thumb with a hammer or hearing someone lie about you. It usually centers on self and may come from such things as someone transgressing your rights (as in a reckless motorist cutting you off in rush hour traffic) or violating you personally (as in a coworker stealing your idea and claiming it as his or her own). Unholy anger responds in ways that are belittling, reckless, thoughtless, and destructive.

Acceptable anger for Christians, on the other hand, reacts against moral evil and injustice in our world. It may be a proper Christian response to unrighteousness. It does not result from attempting to correct a violation of personal rights as much as from attempting to rectify a violation of God's laws. It reacts against the triumph of evil in a particular situation. Jesus became angry with the Pharisees during His ministry and at the folks operating the money tables in the Temple area.

Anger can be a normal human response as with all of our emotions. We cannot keep ourselves from feeling emotions; they just happen to be the way we feel at a point in time. We must, however, guard the way we handle our emotions. We must come to terms with what we are feeling and find ways to respond appropriately with self-control. For as Colley Cibber stated, "He that strives not to stem his anger's tide does a wild horse without a bridle ride."[5]

12. *"I used to have a problem with my mind straying from the subject at hand, but not since the Holy Spirit filled me. He keeps me right on task."*

I've heard this all of my life from my peers and from my university students. Most of us struggle at times with an unruly mind. We're trying to concentrate on the pastor's sermon when, like an elementary school hall monitor, we catch our concentration wandering down some deserted hallway. We may think about a crying baby at the back of the church, the pastor's ugly tie, last night's dinner, or what we will do as soon as the long service ends. Perhaps it's wishful thinking, but most of us desperately want an easy fix for our wandering minds. Some place their hope in holiness and advertise unrealistic claims.

Dwelling on the pastor's ugly tie is a rather harmless exercise. Our minds sometimes wander, on another level, into more dangerous territory. This trip does not start with relaxed consecration but with Satan's suggestions. Thoughts enter our minds about past sinful experiences, about possible indulgences at nightclubs, casinos, or bars, about copying sinful behaviors of others. These suggestions about possible courses of action do not equal sin. They become sin when we dwell on them, long to fulfill them in our lives, or rationalize ways to justify such actions. Immediate expulsion from our mind is our best strategy. You cannot keep Satan from flying over your property with an advertising banner streaming from the tail of his plane, but you don't have to let him land in your backyard and serve him a soft drink.

I heard an advertisement last night on the radio about an amazing product. The ad said I could eat whatever I wanted to eat, take their pill at bedtime, and lose weight while I slept. Send me a case of those pills today!

How absurd! If I want to lose weight, I must discipline my eating and exercise habits. No simple shortcuts, like taking magic pills, will melt my extra pounds away. The same is true with a straying mind. Only discipline and self-control bring better concentration, not a deeper walk with God. By the way, I think the older I get the more trouble I have disciplining my concentration. So, keep your ugly ties away from me!

13. *"Holiness replaced all my desires for material possessions with spiritual goals."*

On the surface this sounds virtuous. However, followed to its logical conclusion, it makes little sense. A young friend of mine once made this claim then shared with me his plans for the future. He planned to quit his job, sell his car, move out of his apartment, and pursue only spiritual concerns. I never understood how he could live without income or a roof over his head, but he sounded extremely spiritual.

A life of holiness does not disqualify you from earning an income or owning a home, car, and personal possessions. It does mean you must be a responsible steward of your money and possessions.

You cannot keep Satan from flying over your property with an advertising banner streaming from the tail of his plane, but you don't have to let him land in your backyard and serve him a soft drink.

It means pursuing a balanced life of work, ministry, and relaxation. It means living within your means so that your house and car payments do not control your life. It means not defining your personhood or worth by the possessions you own. And it means not letting material possessions come between you and God or His call on your life. So, can we escape all association with material possessions to pursue only spiritual goals? Not likely.

14. *"Holiness solved my fashion dilemma."*

You've got to love this one! Some folks think our fellowship with God should show itself to the world by a particular mode of dress. Some holiness people even make their particular clothing selections a required uniform for God's acceptance. These uniforms most often reflect popular fashion of former generations. *Old-fashioned* equals *holy* to them. Some of them cover every body part except face and hands. Does holiness require such strict standards of dress? No.

Holiness does speak to the fashion question. In representing God and His cause to the world, we should dress in such a way that we do not call attention to ourselves. Sort of different, huh? Don't create a diversion to our message of good news. Such attention can come by dressing in an extreme manner, that is, flashy, old-fashioned, old and dirty, weird, unstylish, or highly expensive.

Stay away from the extremes of the fashion parade.

We usually make an immediate connection between expensive clothes and pride. However, some people pride themselves in how poorly or oddly they look. The latter is just as bad as the former. When people look at us, we should draw attention to ourselves as representatives of Christ, not as fashion statements.

Rules of dress differ from region to region in each country and change constantly. So holiness directives cannot be too prescriptive. General ideas include modest, reasonable price, sensible, neat, and clean. Stay away from extreme ends of the fashion parade.

15. *"Now that I'm sanctified, I no longer struggle with doubts or fears about anything in life."*

One Sunday a few years ago while teaching my Sunday School class, I led the group in discussing the doubts and fears that sometimes plague Christians. We talked about fear of tornadoes, inner-city gangs, big dogs, mountain cliffs, and spiders.

We talked about doubts of whether we'd said the right thing in a particular situation, responded to our children appropriately, or had done all we knew to do for God. We also talked about the questions that run through our minds when we're going through the dark valleys of life. Questions like, "Where is God?" "Is He listening to my prayers?" "Does He even care about the situation I'm in right now?"

One dear older saint of the class said, "I'm not comfortable with this discussion. I do not think holiness people will ever experience any kind of doubt or fear if they are truly filled with the Holy Spirit."

What can you say after that? She played the "highly spiritual" card. I tried to show how these types of doubts, fears, and questions are a normal part of life, even a sanctified believer's life. I don't think I convinced her of my position.

Lest you think this belief exists only among the senior saints, let me tell you what I heard a 30-year-old man say just last week. He told me if I truly had faith in God, I wouldn't be afraid of the tornadoes that frequently drop out of our skies. I do trust God, but I also head for the basement when the funnel clouds pass overhead!

I strongly believe holiness does not calm all of our doubts and fears about life. Many things in life remain uncertain. It's true we should not be afraid of God or doubt our salvation. However, sanctification does not dehumanize us. If you didn't like spiders as a sinner, you probably won't like them as a saint. It's better to dialogue with God about your doubts and questions than to deny their existence or suppress them into the realm of the unspeakable. God would rather hear our honesty than watch us suffer in silent denial of our human qualities.

Can You Believe Them?

So, that wraps up our countdown of some of the more popular false advertising claims of holiness folks. We didn't explore everything out there, but we covered the waterfront. When you hear such pious claims as these, can you believe them? Not if you want to keep your sanity and your close relationship with God. If you get caught up in any of these traps, you grow frustrated with your Christian walk and become too discouraged to carry on. So stay close to Scripture and the Lord and let such claims blow on by.

Fast Takes

1. We've grown so accustomed to the exaggerations of false advertising that we automatically discount most of their claims.

2. The church has more than its share of false advertisements of what holiness will do for an individual.

3. Such unrealistic expectations can make us let our guard down against Satan and his evil work.

4. Such claims can lead to frustration and discouragement if our Christian walk does not measure up to promised standards.

Think About This . . .

1. What are some of the most popular unrealistic claims you have heard about holiness?

2. What other claims have you heard?

3. Why do you think people make such exaggerated claims?

4. What danger do such unrealistic claims pose to those who think this is the true nature of holiness?

5. How can people who live holy lives still be tempted?

6. Look over the list of what holiness does not do for a person. Think through your personal response to each claim.

> I have learned to place myself before God
> every day as a vessel to be filled
> with His Holy Spirit. He has filled me
> with the blessed assurance that He,
> as the everlasting God, has guaranteed
> His own work in me.
> —*Andrew Murray*[1]

11

THE TEST-DRIVE

Try It Out

Sometimes we see a car advertisement in the newspaper or on television that piques our interest in a new car. So, we visit the dealership, examine the car from top to bottom, kick the tires (for whatever reason people do that), and look under the hood. Then, we participate in one more essential ritual of car shopping: the test-drive. We want to be sure the car performs as advertised. We want to feel the way it handles on the road; we want to test its limits.

Sue and I always buy our cars from our good friend Sam. He has gotten our cars for us for nearly two decades. When I'm in the market for a car, I just call him and tell him what kind of vehicle I want. In a couple of weeks, he parks the car I've described in our driveway and leaves it for us to test-drive. We plan to stop by Sam's dealership in a couple of days and sign papers on the car if we decide to keep it. A few years ago something went wrong with our plan, however. Sam brought us a white, four-door sedan just as we requested. We liked it and decided to keep it. But we got busy, then Sam got busy, so the paperwork fell by the wayside. We actually drove the car for a month before we closed the deal. Now that's what I call a test-drive!

Let's apply this thought to our subject. Holiness is God's incredible plan: a plan He formulated even before He created us. The Bible speaks clearly about God's will for us to live holy lives. It gives us many examples of men and women who lived holy lives. Church history provides examples from the past up to today.

What can we honestly expect from a holiness lifestyle? When we take this biblical notion on a test-drive, here are some of the outcomes we can expect to find in our lives.

Holiness on a Test-Drive

God does many wonderful things in our spiritual walk with Him as we bring His plan to reality in our lives. We must always remember that God works with us as individuals, so no two believers' experiences with God will be identical. God also works with a timetable based on our abilities to respond to His direction. So, the following observations generally represent the kinds of directions God takes us, not cookie-cutter prescriptions of how each of us will look the minute God's Spirit takes full control of our lives.

> *God works with us as individuals, so no two believers' experiences with God will be absolutely identical.*

As we discussed in chapter 9, God's timetable is seeker-sensitive to our need and to our openness to Him working with us. Never get discouraged because growth is not as quick as you would like.

1. *Holiness makes us more sensitive to the Holy Spirit's leading in our lives.*

We become more aware of God's direction, more in tune with the gentle voice guiding our choices. This fulfills the images that God gave His prophets about how things would be when the Holy Spirit filled followers. Review God's words to Isaiah (44:3), Jeremiah (31:31-33), Ezekiel (36:23, 25-27), and Joel (2:28-29). Not only do these passages speak of heart cleansing from the spiritual infection that hinders our progress, but they also speak of an internal awareness of God's will and plan for us.

God only asks that we seek Him and welcome His presence in our lives more than anything. With that open invitation, He willingly gives us new insight for daily living.

2. *Holiness gives us a new and deeper love for God and others.*

Love becomes an affection and a principle of life for us. We seek to love God more than anything. Whenever we see something else taking that supreme place in our lives, we quickly lower its position and restore God to first place. We begin to see people as God sees them. We genuinely care about their needs and find ways to meet those needs.

The driving force of this love is not a great deal of extra effort on our part but the love of God flowing through us. That's why we call it "perfect love," not because it responds perfectly in every situation but because it comes from God and reaches to His hurting world. It contains no mixture of selfish ambition. We strive to love others the way the Father loves His Son and the way the Son loves us. That kind of love can't go unnoticed, for as George Herbert said, "Love and a cough cannot be hid."[2]

We become channels through whom His love flows. Only this explains our ability to love our enemies, the unlovely, and the unlovable. We love them with a love God gives us. First Cor. 13 describes this kind of love. This chapter serves a greater good than simply providing a beautiful poem for Christian weddings. It outlines the way God's love works through us in the power of the Holy Spirit.

3. *Holiness gives us a new level of humility and awareness of the grace of God at work in us.*

Perhaps the chief enemy to humility is self-centeredness. Self keenly tracks personal accomplishments. As one of my friends fondly says, "It's hard to be humble when you're so good." When the Holy Spirit takes full control of our lives, He replaces self-centeredness with Christ-centeredness.

It's a lot easier to be humble when you properly realize that everything you are and everything you hope to become are gifts of God's grace. You'll find no room for pride in that mind-set. That's why apologies come more quickly. That's why we're not overly concerned about who gets the credit in a team effort we participate in. We are more sensitive to our human frailty and more aware of our constant need for God's help. We also admit our performance won't always be flawless.

Spiritual humility implies no self-deprecation or lack of self-worth. It does not call us to always put ourselves down in conversation or underestimate our talents. Rather, it gives us a more realistic view of ourselves.

From a Christian perspective, a realistic view is quite positive, for it emphasizes who we are by God's grace. The Holy Spirit's work in us should actually contribute to our self-worth and respect. Freedom from sin and empowerment from God give us reason to celebrate God's work in us. A proper understanding of all this leaves us humbly dependent on God.

4. *Holiness gives us a new level of spiritual sensitivity.*

This new spiritual sensitivity helps us recognize temptation, faults, and sin for what they really are. Temptation is simply Satan offering suggestions for us to fulfill legitimate needs in ungodly ways. It implies no slippage from God or hunger to return to old sinful paths. We say, "Thanks, but no thanks" and move on down the road. Remember N. P. Willis's reminder, "No degree of temptation justifies any degree of sin."[3]

Make up your mind, before temptation knocks, that you won't yield to the suggestion—then don't.

Faults plague us as fallen creatures living in a fallen world. We accept the fact that we have finite knowledge and reasoning abilities. Therefore, our judgments are not always correct. We forget things, confuse details, get sick, need rest, have weaknesses, and lose our concentration. We don't have an excuse for these things; they're simply human faults. All of us differ in our combination of faults, but all of us have abundant faults. A terrible error occurs when we call these faults sin. Never! Sin is a willful disobedience to God's known will.

It's also a terrible error to call sin anything other than what it is—sin. We sometimes try to hide sin behind the *fault* excuse. It won't work. Too often holiness people make no provision in their thinking for sin to creep into their lives. If it does, they don't know how to deal with it, so they dismiss it as less than it is. In this way, they deceive themselves and fall short of God's will. Holiness's new sensitivity gives us new ears to hear the voice of the Holy Spirit, who helps us sort through a proper understanding of temptation, faults, and sin.

5. *Holiness encourages us to seek every opportunity to serve God.*

Without question, a holy life brings a life of service. Holiness is love dressed in work clothes. We seek ways to invest our energies and abilities in building the kingdom of God and relieving the pain and suffering of those in need. Holiness does not call us to withdraw from our hurting world; it sends us to serve. For as Dag Hammarskjöld said, "The road to holiness necessarily passes through the world of action."[4]

God does not clean our hearts and lives to place us on a fireplace mantle like some treasured trophy. He cleans us up and screws our heads on straight so we can go out and offer God's comfort. God doesn't comfort us to make us comfortable but to make us comforters. Our holiness ancestors heavily involved themselves in social reform issues of their society. We must get involved too.

We give all we can and do all we can whether anyone notices it or offers praise. We don't seek attention or reward. We do not need our accomplishments listed in the church bulletin, either. We died to that when we died with Christ. We offer our service as a thanksgiving offering to God for all He has done for us. We serve because He first served us. The picture of Jesus with water basin and towel in hand, washing His disciples' feet motivates us to follow His example.

Selfish ambition no longer drives us to spend all of our time and energy pampering ourselves. The Spirit brings us freedom to serve selflessly wherever God needs our help. And, in everything we do, we seek to glorify God. As Mother Teresa put it, "Our little acts of obedience give us the occasion of proving our love for Him."[5]

6. *Holiness strengthens our resolve to resist the world's attempt to squeeze us into its mold.*

It's no accident—we're not picking up stray signals from our culture calling us to conform. We've been targeted with a bull's-eye on our backs. Culture has a plan to order our lives. It seeks to select the clothes we wear, the way we cut our hair, the music we listen to, the food we eat, and the way we spend our extra time and money. It wants to tell us how to think and feel about every possible subject. That's why advertisers spend billions of dollars. If we refuse to fall within prescribed guidelines we may be labeled intolerant, bigoted, and politically incorrect.

> **We need to be Teflon-coated Christians.**

We discussed culture's strategy in chapter 6 when we looked at the second half of Rom. 12:2. God knows all about the world's plan to squeeze us into certain molds. That's why He warns us against it. So, what do we do? We can't withdraw from society to live in caves buried deeply in the woods. We must rub shoulders with the world every day. No, retreat is not the answer; holiness provides us with protective insulation to keep the corrupting influences of the world from corrupting us.

Jesus urged us in John 14 to be in the world but not of it. Politicians are often described as wearing Teflon coats. It means media criticism does not stick to them; it rolls off like water off a Teflon skillet. We, too, need to be Teflon-coated Christians. We do have to live here, but we don't think and act like the world.

The Holy Spirit offers us daily guidance in how to accomplish this tedious task. The task remains tedious because culture changes constantly. The only certainty: things will change soon. Not everything in society is sinful or harmful to spiritual life. The Spirit must help us analyze daily choices to decide which ones are crucial to our spiritual growth and which are trivial. We cannot afford to spend a great deal of time on the trivial choices, nor can we afford to trivialize the crucial choices. Ultimately the more we're attracted to Christ, the less we're attracted to the world.

7. *Holiness brings our greatest fulfillment in life from finding and doing God's will.*

I know that sounds strange. Society programs us to think we find fulfillment by doing what we want to do. That's the message of all those self-help books at the local bookstore; it's the message of talk show interviews on television. In fact, Ayn Rand developed an entire philosophy of selfishness. You'll find it explained in her book *The Virtue of Selfishness.*

She argues that you only have full knowledge of what one person in this world wants—you. Therefore, you should live to please yourself.[6]

We are satisfied and yet hungry at the same time.

That's not the philosophy of a committed Christian: quite the opposite. We want God's will accomplished in our lives more than anything. This works so well because fulfillment in life is not a goal to seek, it is a result of correct priorities and good choices. Like C. S. Lewis said, "If you live for the next world, you get this one in the deal; but if you live only for this world, you lose them both."[7]

I have a friend who divorced her husband because she no longer found the fulfillment she wanted in married life. Her husband had not been unfaithful or neglected her and their children. She simply grew tired of the daily stresses of the home. She thought her life would be more fulfilled without him. I do not think she has been pleased with the results of her decision. She certainly did not find the fulfillment she sought because she sought it through a sinful choice.

On the other hand, the committed Christian who spends every day immersed in pleasing God finds fulfillment beyond description. As George W. Truett reminds, "To know the will of God is the greatest knowledge, to find the will of God is the greatest discovery, and to do the will of God is the greatest achievement."[8] In the end, we're much happier doing God's will than our own.

8. *Holiness gives us a hunger for more of God's presence and influence in our lives.*

An amazing paradox emerges when believers' lives are totally dedicated to God. We are full and yet seeking to be filled at the same time. We are satisfied and yet hungry. How can that be? Because while God totally fills and satisfies us, He also urges us to seek a deeper relationship with Him. For example, when I drink a sweet soda drink my thirst is quenched and I want to drink more at the same time. The more I drink, the more I want to drink.

Jesus said, "Blessed are those who hunger and thirst for righteousness, for they will be filled" (Matt. 5:6). However, the filling creates a deeper hunger and thirst for more of God than we presently know. That's why we read His Word and pray so often. We enjoy being in His presence, and we find the hunger of our hearts filled with His completeness. We do not need to wait for heaven to experience His presence, but when we arrive there we will have a healthy appetite for more of Him than we could ever experience here on earth.

9. *Holiness produces the fruit of the Spirit in us.*

God's desired fruit in our lives includes love, joy, peace, patience, kindness, goodness, faithfulness, gentleness, and self-control (Gal. 5:22). These qualities are in short supply in society. God counts on us to bring a bumper crop of these fruits in our world. Laurence Housman said a saint is someone who makes these virtues attractive.[9]

They certainly are great virtues, but can we produce these fruits just by reading this scriptural list and telling ourselves to produce? Never! That points to a big problem in the church. Christians often try to produce the fruits of the Spirit by trying harder. They strain and strive to generate the fruits. They often end up not with healthy fruit but with frustration. Why? Because they strive to do it by their own strength.

Jesus offered a helpful reminder in John 15:1-2 when He explained that the Father is the gardener, Jesus is the vine, and we are the branches. Branches do not produce fruit by themselves. They remain attached to the vine and are cared for by the gardener. Together the gardener and the vine supply all the elements necessary for quality fruit. As God's Holy Spirit fills us, we produce His fruit naturally as a result of living daily in God's presence.

I used to think the fruit of the Spirit resulted from lots of effort and determination. Now I realize it comes from a greater openness to God's grace. I cannot produce by myself, but I can make myself available for God to produce in me.

10. *Holiness makes Christ the centerpiece of life.*

The Father gave us a full-color picture of himself in His Son, Jesus Christ. Everything Jesus said and did in His earthly ministry reflected God's perfect plan—His original intention for all humanity. Adam and his offspring missed that plan; Christ got it right (Rom. 5:12-19). So, now we have an illustration of how that plan looks in daily operation. We have an example, a model.

That's what the writer to the Hebrews had in mind when he said, "Let us fix our eyes on Jesus, the author and perfecter of our faith" (12:2). Holiness is about a lot of things. But holiness is more about Christlikeness that anything else.

A Realistic List

So there you have it: a test-drive of holiness in daily living. A much more realistic list than the false claims we considered in the last chapter, right? I get excited about this list. It takes holiness out of the realm of the otherworldly and places it in my lap.

Holiness isn't an overnight quick fix for all my faults and shortcomings. But in bringing me closer to God, it allows Him to help me with these areas in far better ways than I can do by my own power. I like the way G. Campbell Morgan summarized true expectations for holiness:

1. Not inability to sin, but ability not to sin
2. Not freedom from temptation, but power to overcome temptation
3. Not infallible judgment, but earnest and honest endeavor to follow the higher wisdom
4. Not deliverance from infirmities of the flesh, but triumph over all bodily affliction
5. Not exemption from conflict, but victory through conflict
6. Not freedom from liability and falling, but gracious ability to prevent falling
7. Not the end of progress, but deliverance from standing still[10]

I'm learning that God has far more patience with me and hope for me than I sometimes have. If He's willing to continue to work with me, who am I to quit trying? More than anything, He wants to bring me to conformity to the image of His Son, Jesus Christ. So, we'll keep working.

Fast Takes

1. God works with each believer on an individual basis. So, His timetable and operation in each of our lives will be somewhat different.
2. Holiness helps us realize the Holy Spirit's work in our lives to make us more loving, humble, and spiritually sensitive.
3. While we actively work in our world, we do not conform to its ways.
4. Doing God's will brings great fulfillment, satisfaction, and spiritual fruit.
5. More than anything, holiness seeks to make us more like Christ.

Think About This . . .

1. How does the Holy Spirit increase our sensitivity toward Him as we open ourselves more fully to God?
2. Why is holiness often imaged in terms of increased love for God and others?
3. Why should holiness increase our level of humility?
4. Explain how we live in the world without adopting its worldview or mind-set.
5. Why is a person most happy and fulfilled in life when he or she is doing God's will?
6. Holiness conversation talks about being satisfied in God and yet hungering for more of God. Which is it—satisfaction or deeper hunger?
7. In what ways can we be like Christ?

> It is not a question of who or what you are,
> but whether God controls you.
> —*J. Wilbur Chapman*[1]

STEVE: A CASE STUDY

One Sunday Evening

Sue and I walked into our church sanctuary and routinely sat down one Sunday evening in September. In a minute Steve, our university student body president, and his fiancé, Stephanie, sat beside us. We visited for a few minutes, then the service started. I don't remember the pastor's message that evening. However, at the end of the service he invited folks to pray at the altar if they had a special need they wanted to bring to God. Steve stepped forward to pray.

Steve had been a good friend of our family for many years; I knew him well. In fact, he had been a good friend to our son Brent since early childhood. I thought I might help him in praying for his need, so I also went forward and knelt across from Steve at the altar. His fiancé and brother James knelt on either side of him. I had no idea I was about to participate in one of the most interesting spiritual experiences of my life.

Steve had grown up in a Christian home and had followed Jesus Christ since he was seven years old. He lived an exemplary Christian life. He was a good role model to other university students. So I figured he came to pray about some snag he had encountered on his spiritual journey.

The word *snag* doesn't even begin to describe his dilemma. After we prayed together, I asked Steve if I could pray with him about any specific issue. Steve opened his heart to Stephanie, James, and me.

Where the Search Began

Steve had attended a denominational youth conference with more than 7,000 other teenagers during the summer after he graduated from high school. The event involved a week of special singers, seminars, and speakers all focused on Christian discipleship. In the last Sunday morning service of the conference, Steve sensed God speaking to him in a new way. He didn't hear an audible voice, but he recognized God's presence. God simply asked, "What about ministry?" A rather short, pointed question.

Without seriously examining the question, Steve replied, "I'm open." Steve neither understood the question nor its implications for him. The conference ended; Steve returned home with good memories and an Arizona tan.

God simply asked, "What about ministry?"

Three years had passed between the youth conference and our Sunday night prayer. During that time Steve told his parents, grandparents, brother, and fiancé about God's question playing over and over in his mind. They all contemplated with Steve what it meant for his life. He had sensed God's presence in chapel services, Bible studies, and university classes. So he hadn't tried to run from God's question. He just didn't know what it meant for him.

Still Searching

During his freshman year of college, Steve had traveled with Sue and me on our ministry trip to Brazil. One night Steve questioned several of us at length about how God's call to ministry felt. We all described our calls to him. Steve processed everything we said. Unfortunately, I think we created more questions and fears for him because he hoped his call from God didn't involve pastoring a local congregation like ours did. Steve ended his freshman year of college still contemplating the question, "What about ministry?"

Steve returned for his sophomore year of college, determined to answer God's question. He decided to experiment with every form of ministry except one. He refused to even think about a call to the pastorate. That year he ministered in student government, in a freshman mentor program, and led a hall of dormitory guys as their resident assistant. He poured himself as heavily as he could into people's lives. This experimentation with various forms of ministry continued through his junior year. However, through that entire two-year process he remained unsure about an appropriate answer to God's question.

As Steve entered his senior year of college he decided it was time to bring closure to this question that had trailed him for three years. For one thing, he was tired of thinking about it. For another, he couldn't keep changing his major course of study. You see, throughout this entire process of experimenting with ministry options, Steve had also experimented with career options and changed his major with each new experiment. This was not the usual approach for Steve, since his life pattern had been to decide a plan and stick with it, the way he zeroed in on Stephanie his first day on the university campus and dated her exclusively until he married her.

Steve first thought ministry for him meant being a doctor, so he began college as a premed major. Then he switched to physical therapy. From there he explored a nursing major. Then back to premed. Finally, he settled on a sociology major, planning to become a social worker. All worthy careers; all a million miles from pastoring a church, the one thing he subconsciously resisted! As he put it, "I wanted a profession that would be ministry without being a minister."

That Sunday night as we prayed with Steve, we all soon discovered exactly what the God-asked question meant for him. Three years of contemplation ended. Three years of seeking and striving ceased.

Looking back on that night, Steve said, "I didn't want to say no to God, but I couldn't deal with the question any longer in my own strength. I knew what needed to happen: I needed to depend completely on God. But I couldn't seem to make it work in my life. I decided to let all my defenses down that night and drop the struggle. I had to face each issue plaguing me and deal with them. Even though I never said no to God, I implied it with my decision. That had to end."

> *I decided to let all my defenses down that night and drop the struggle.*

The Issues

The pattern of our prayer involved praying about a particular issue until he surrendered it to God, then moving on to the next one. Some issues took longer to resolve than others. However, each appeared as an insurmountable mountain staring Steve in the face. What issues haunted him? Here is a summary of each struggle in Steve's words.

1. "If I agree unconditionally to God's terms and He calls us to pastoral ministry, we will be poor."

2. "If we are poor, we won't have enough money to raise our children. My parents sacrificed to give James and me everything we needed. They did everything they could to help us. If I can't follow their example with my children, it will be a slap in my parents' faces for all they have done for my brother and me."

3. "If we are in pastoral ministry, we won't be able to send our children to a Christian college like we had the privilege of attending."

4. "What if we pastor hard churches and everything goes wrong?"

5. "What if difficult church members make life hard for my wife or children? I don't want to be responsible to God for losing them."

6. "What if my wife or parents don't go along with God's call to pastoral ministry? They might resist it. What will I do then?"

If I'm fully open to God, I will lose control of my life.

7. "If I decide this on my own, I might threaten my relationship with my wife and parents. It's as if they have nothing to say about the direction I take my life."

8. "If God controls my life, I will run into conflicts with my wife and parents when God leads me to do something they don't understand or agree with. I don't want to live in conflict with any family members."

9. "I'm a people pleaser. If God calls the shots in my life, I have to do what He says, not what others want me to do. This will create conflict. Jesus found himself in many conflicts with people. I don't want that."

10. "What will my major in college be? I've already had five majors; none of them seem right for me."

11. "If I agree to pastoral ministry, I'll have to attend seminary. Since I wasn't a religion major in college, I won't be properly prepared for seminary. Thus, I won't do well. I don't want to fail."

12. "If I'm fully open to God, I will lose control of my life. I'm a very independent person. I don't want to be owned by anyone else. I don't want to give anyone the power to completely control me."

BINGO! The crux of the entire struggle. Like a builder with plans spread across the table counting construction costs, Steve saw the entire span of his life spread before him as he counted the cost of complete openness to God. He saw himself declaring bankruptcy in light of God's challenge. In a very real sense, Steve came to terms with the possibility of writing his entire future off as a total loss. At least, that's the way he saw it.

Finally, after an hour and a half of struggle, Steve rested in the resolve: "I quit. I'm fully open to whatever God wants for my life. I don't care any longer about any of my concerns. I know God has a plan, and I know that plan will work. Being in that plan and having that call mean more to me than all the rest. I want God; that's all."

In that moment something happened in Steve. I felt privileged to have witnessed it. Nothing emotional or physical happened, but just a sense of rest and peace swept over him. The God-asked question had its answer. Steve owned the call. No, that's not right; the call owned him. Steve remembers, "I felt blessed, not whipped."

A Closer Look

So what was happening between Steve and God in that three-year period from the youth conference until we prayed together? Was God playing cat and mouse with Steve? Every time Steve nearly figured God's plan for his life, did God hide it in a new mouse hole just out of his reach? Or was God placing His plan like a carrot on a stick just out of Steve's grasp? Steve certainly appeared to be open to God's direction throughout those three years. He certainly sought diligently enough to locate God's will. What created the problem, then?

Consider that at no point did Steve ever openly say no to God. In fact, he appeared to be open to divine direction as he searched through a maze of ministry opportunities and career options. Like trying on an armload of new clothes at a mall clothing store, Steve tried on various ministries and careers and lived with each of them long enough to know that they did not fit. While they brought some level of fulfillment to his life, they did not completely answer the God-asked question.

Something of a virtual reality played out in his mind as he came to terms with these worst-case scenarios.

That question repeatedly surfaced and remained unanswered. Each time it surfaced it brought a new level of frustration, because each time he seemed to hear, "No, this is not ministry for you." Steve became increasingly frustrated with his shrinking pool of options. He also became more frustrated with his own lack of strength, his inability to do the ministry he felt God called him to do. He felt increasingly inadequate and unable to do whatever God had in mind for him.

Each of the 12 issues Steve brought before God explored a different avenue of his fear about possible worst-case scenarios regarding the future. It also exposed Steve's fear of inadequately dealing with each situation should his worst fears materialize. To those of us looking at Steve's struggle from the outside, most of his fears appear unrealistic. However, to Steve they were very real. A virtual reality played out in his mind as he came to terms with these worst-case scenarios. This entire process involved counting the cost of total discipleship.

By God's enabling strength, Steve successfully climbed over each of these obstacles until he reached the last one. It proved to be the largest mountain, for it contained the heart of the entire matter.

Throughout Steve's life and even at the Arizona youth conference, he willingly gave God every key on the ring of his life except for one. That one key did not appear to be a big issue; it only opened one lock in his heart. But that lock contained the one thing he unconsciously feared the most. Behind that one lock lurked the possibility that God's plan for Steve might include pastoral ministry.

God pointed to the one key Steve hid for himself.

That's why over a three-year period Steve continued to recommit all the other keys to God. He showed his openness to God's direction in his sensitive willingness to change his major, not once or twice, but five times. And with each of these changes came the hope that God would be pleased with his dedication and would suggest no further commitment necessary at that time.

Ultimately, the entire three-year journey came down to a Sunday evening in which God's original question, "What about ministry?" expanded to ask, "What about pastoral ministry?" God pointed to the one key Steve hid for himself. God wanted that key too.

As with all of us, Steve came face-to-face with the realization that God can never be satisfied with a 98 percent commitment. He requires 100 percent of our availability to grant to us the ultimate satisfaction of being centered in His will—which we all desperately need. Remember, too, that for as long as he could recall, Steve had attempted, to the best of his ability, to remain open to God. His attendance at church, Bible reading, prayer, and the pursuit of a Christian higher education all reflected the reality of that commitment. His involvement in various campuswide ministries also spoke to his openness to ministry. At no point in Steve's entire life did he flagrantly rebel or quench God's Spirit. As far as he could tell in God's dealings with him, he remained forthright and sensitive.

Steve's search finally reached a point at which he craved an immediate resolution. He tired of trying one ministry and then another only to come up empty-handed. So, everything considered, Steve ultimately reached a critical conclusion. His conclusion applies to us as well. For while the struggles may differ and issues take turns based on our unique personalities, they all somehow seem to come back to that one question: "Who's in control?"

The lowest common denominator always remains, as Steve put it, "I don't want to be owned by anyone else. I don't want to give anyone the power to completely control me." Yet, ultimately that is exactly what God wants. That is precisely the price we each must pay.

It happens a little differently in each of us. However, in one way or another, we all see our lives spread before us like legal papers spread across the kitchen table. We must count the cost of complete openness to God. Sooner or later, we reach the same conclusion as Steve, the declaration of personal bankruptcy in light of God's challenge. We all face the awareness that we may have to write our entire future off as a total loss, in our perspectives. Are we willing to partner with God to the degree that we're OK with that? Finally, we each come to that moment of saying with Steve, "I quit. I'm fully open to whatever God wants in my life. I want God and that's all."

It's not always an emotional decision. It should, however, always be a calculated and reasoned decision after we say everything we feel we need to say to God. The final conclusion to the matter—God's call owns us. But as we consecrate ourselves to Him, we find no sense of defeat, loss, or surrender to something undesirable. Rather, we can accept the resolution that wherever God leads us we will follow. We know He has our best interests in mind and that God's plan will prove to be what's best for us as well.

> *The final conclusion to the matter— God's call owns us.*

An Update

Two years have passed since Stephanie, James, and I prayed together on that Sunday evening. I have talked with Steve about it several times. We've laughed at the nature of some of his issues. We've rejoiced in the lessons God has taught Steve during these past two years.

After Steve reflected on his new commitment to God, did he feel a call to pastoral ministry? He certainly did! Since his college credits encompassed a variety of majors, he used his senior year to complete the major in which he had the most hours—sociology. All of that broad-based education won't hurt him. It will give him a broader perspective from which to minister.

After Steve graduated from our university he moved on to seminary and has just completed his first year of ministry preparation. How does he feel about seminary? As you might expect, he loves every minute of every class. Why might you expect that? Because he's centered in God's plan for his life. I love what he said the other day, "God knew I would like seminary all along; it's a total fit."

I asked Steve to summarize what he has learned about the three years of struggling to answer God's question and about the two years since he's come to terms with the answer. Here's what he said,

Conformity to Christ takes a yes at every point along the way. We're people in process. More than the moment of time when I surrendered all at the altar is my daily dying to self. Daily I choose to say yes or no to God's involvement in my life.

Every little thing counts. I must remember that. Every little decision counts. We want God to zap us instantly into sainthood. It's a much longer process than that. During the hard times I know it's for my benefit. I enjoy the good times and am thankful for them. Overall it comes down to one thing—obedience. You endure the hard times and enjoy the good times all with obedience.

Theology in Reverse

This chapter summarizes everything I want to say in this book. It's theology in reverse. Rather than trying to make a logical or biblical case for a doctrine, then following it with an illustration, this chapter has explored a real experience bringing the following conclusions that represent the ways God works with all of us on our spiritual journeys. For while we each relate to God individually, we also share commonalties, including:

1. A complete openness to God's voice
2. A current walk with Christ
3. Participating in all the means of grace God provides for our spiritual growth
4. Sensitivity to the Lord's direction
5. Counting the cost of full openness to God
6. Working through the issues that block our way
7. A moment when we decide to give God all of the keys, though it costs us everything
8. Allowing God's call to fully own us
9. The process of maturity
10. Obeying God as a lifestyle

Fast Takes

1. Christian discipleship requires openness to hear and obey the voice of God.
2. At some point along a believer's journey, God will challenge us to a deeper consecration than we have ever known.
3. This challenge requires 100 percent commitment.
4. When we agree to God's terms, we rest knowing that wherever God leads, we will follow.

Think About This . . .

1. How has your personal spiritual journey been similar to Steve's?
2. How has your personal spiritual journey been different from Steve's?
3. Why did God's question to Steve take three years to answer?

4. Why do you think Steve subconsciously resisted pastoral ministry?

5. Why does God always zero in on our final little stronghold of personal autonomy?

6. Why is counting the cost of total consecration so important?

7. Why does total consecration bring such peace and contentment?

> A true and faithful Christian does not make
> holy living a mere incidental thing.
> As the business of the soldier is to fight,
> so the business of the Christian is
> to be like Christ.
> —*Jonathan Edwards*[1]

13
CHRISTLIKENESS

Like Father, like Son

Our son Brent graduated last spring from the university where Sue and I teach. To commemorate the event, Sue hung a new picture frame on the living room wall. The frame holds two graduation photos: one of me when I graduated from college, and one of Brent at his graduation. One glance tells an entire story. Brent looks much as I looked when I was his age. But, more importantly, the smile and stance speak of how much like me Brent became. Without a conscious effort, he emulated me in many ways. In fact, people often comment after being around us, "There's no doubt whose son he is!"

How did that happen? Quietly, slowly over the period of an entire life the son began to look, sound, and act like his father. This emulation requires no planning or effort. It happens naturally through the give-and-take of life. God knew that's the way life works. That's why He incorporated this phenomenon into His plan for us.

Reviewing God's Plan

We began our study of holiness by looking at our holy God and His desire for us to be holy as well. We talked about the Father's dream and plan for our lives. We then spoke of the damaging effect of sin and rebellion against God. With sin came a bent in our nature to prefer our will over God's will. We labeled it as an infection that plagues us all. We moved on to talk about God's cure for that infection, a cure that restores us to God's original intention for us—a vital experience and relationship with Him. Next, we explored the claims of holiness, both false and true. The false claims rival the best infomercials on television. The true claims not only represent a realistic plan but also work in life's grind.

God designed a masterful plan for us. But He needed more than a good game plan. He needed an example to set before us. He needed a picture of the goal, a picture we could stick on the refrigerator door and look at when we reach for a cold drink. So, He did just that. He lovingly framed us a picture of His Son and said, "Become like Him." That's what Paul meant when he said, "For those God foreknew he also predestined to be conformed to the likeness of his Son, that he might be the firstborn among many brothers" (Rom. 8:29).

A Picture of the Goal

That's the goal of holiness—Christlikeness. When we consider holiness as it relates to us, it's easy to study the Old Testament symbols and rituals pointing to its intentions. From there we find ourselves turning to the Pauline Epistles for Paul's many analogies and appeals to holiness. If we're not careful, we can get so involved in analogy that we miss the whole point of Scripture's appeal for our holiness. Ultimately, God wants to make us like His Son Jesus Christ.

Holiness seeks to form us in the image of Christ.

Remember Col. 1:27, "To them God has chosen to make known among the Gentiles the glorious riches of this mystery, which is Christ in you, the hope of glory." Paul said he was working with the Galatians "until Christ is formed in you" (Gal. 4:19). Holiness seeks to form us in the image of Christ. We seek to live in such ways that as people get to know us better, they get to know Christ better. That's a lifelong process. Christ lives and works in us as we aim the mirror of our heart toward Him and allow Him to shine His holiness light through us.

As Paul put it, "And we, who with unveiled faces all reflect the Lord's glory, are being transformed into his likeness with ever-increasing glory, which comes from the Lord, who is the Spirit" (2 Cor. 3:18). Peter reminds us that as we do this, we participate in Christ's divine nature. "Through these he has given us his very great and precious promises, so that through them you may participate in the divine nature and escape the corruption in the world caused by evil desires" (2 Pet. 1:4).

We must constantly recall that becoming more like Christ does not bring us a single step closer to earning our salvation. We do not live righteous lives to purchase God's favor. Our right standing with God always remains a free gift from Him. No, we live as God wants us to live and seek to become more like His Son because we love Him and want to honor Him in all we do. How better to express our gratitude for all He has done for us than by seeking to pattern ourselves after Jesus Christ?

Describing the Picture

Trying to describe this incredible picture of God's Son is like trying to capture the majesty of the Grand Canyon with a $5 disposable camera. That doesn't mean we shouldn't take a stab at it, though. Even an imperfect picture beats no picture at all. Here's a thumbnail sketch of how that picture looks.

1. *Jesus loved the Father first and foremost, then He loved us as an outgrowth of their love for each other.*

Jesus' words and deeds throughout His earthly life evidenced those two priorities in His life. He demonstrated daily what He proclaimed in His ministry. "'Love the Lord your God with all your heart and with all your soul and with all your mind.' This is the first and greatest commandment. And the second is like it: 'Love your neighbor as yourself.' All the Law and the Prophets hang on these two commandments" (Matt. 22:37-40).

2. *Jesus had a winsome personality.*

Crowds pressed Him by the thousands. Something about His life and conversation attracted them like metal shavings to a magnet. They wanted to hear what He had to say and see Him in action (John 6:1-2). He helped people feel at ease in His presence. Many people, like Nicodemus, opened up and shared their hearts with Him (3:1-21).

3. *Jesus lived a life of humility.*

Jesus did not put himself down, but He gave himself away to meet others' needs. He even talked about being lowly in spirit as a virtue for us to emulate. "Take my yoke upon you and learn from me, for I am gentle and humble in heart, and you will find rest for your souls" (Matt. 11:29). Once His disciples argued among themselves about which of them was greater. Jesus illustrated the error of their thinking by placing a child among them and stressing the virtue of childlikeness (18:1-5).

When James and John sought to rule with Him in His coming kingdom, Jesus pointed out that those who want to rule over all must become humble servants of all (Mark 10:43-45). Then, at the Last Supper, He washed His disciples' feet as a humble example for us all (John 13:2-16).

4. *Jesus lived a balanced life.*

Jesus worked, rested, spent time with others, took time to be alone,

> *Trying to describe this incredible picture of God's Son is like trying to capture the majesty of the Grand Canyon with a $5 disposable camera.*

He stayed busy, but He knew when to stop and rest.

socialized with saints and sinners, and enjoyed the give-and-take of daily life. He was neither a workaholic nor a man of leisure. He stayed busy, but He knew when to stop and rest.

5. *Jesus had a sense of humor.*

Jesus wasn't always seriously preaching and teaching. He mixed a great deal of humor with His personal conversation and formal messages. He spoke of seeing a splinter while tripping over a large board (Matt. 7:3). He joked about tediously straining a gnat out of a drink then swallowing a camel (23:24). Try to picture those images without laughing!

6. *Jesus had a heart of compassion and gave His hands to compassionate ministry.*

As He walked and talked with the crowds of people who followed Him, Jesus' heart reached out to their hurts and needs. Anyone who came to Jesus found a listening ear and an outstretched hand. He sympathized with people and did what He could to help them (8:14-17).

7. *Jesus lived a life of fairness.*

He defended His disciples when others wrongly accused them but also scolded them when they were wrong (Mark 2:23-28). For example, He criticized Peter when Peter rebuked Jesus for predicting His death but praised Peter for recognizing Him as the Christ, the Son of the living God (Matt. 16:13-23).

8. *Jesus was courteous.*

He spoke with dignity and respect to society's outcasts and those with sinful pasts. People's stations in life did not impress Jesus. He treated the rich, poor, educated, uneducated, important, and disenfranchised all the same. The Jewish male, Jesus, conversed with the Samaritan female in public—a forbidden social practice. At the end of the religious discussion, Jesus led her to a relationship with God (John 4:4-26). He knew everyone needed a relationship with His Father.

9. *Jesus was thoughtful.*

In the confusion of Jesus' arrest in the Garden of Gethsemane, Peter lashed out with his sword and cut off Malchus's ear. Jesus miraculously healed Malchus (Luke 22:50-51).

10. *Jesus paid compliments and showed appreciation.*

Jesus paid a high compliment to a sinful woman and created a social scene at the home of a Pharisee when the woman honored Jesus by anointing His feet with alabaster perfume and wiping them with her hair (7:36-50).

11. *Jesus did not try to create conflict with His enemies, but when it arose He did not run from it.*

The Pharisees, at one point, prepared to do battle with Jesus, so He moved His ministry from Judea, back through Samaria to Galilee (John 4:1-3). However, when the chief priests and teachers of the law tried to trip Him with a trick question, He stood up to them and refused to answer their question (Luke 20:1-8). Another time, Jesus publicly broke a man-made Sabbath rule to make a point with a Pharisee (14:1-5).

> *He did not assume a victim mentality, blame others, or feel sorry for himself.*

12. *Jesus did not contemplate His plight in life and feel sorry for himself.*

He lived with the shame and slander surrounding society's notion of His illegitimate birth. He acknowledged personal rejection by His hometown community. He lived with constant opposition from His enemies. His own brothers and sisters did not honor Him during His ministry. His own disciples did not understand Him most of the time. Yet, He did not assume a victim mentality, blame others, or feel sorry for himself (23:28-31).

13. *Jesus was not vindictive and did not retaliate when others treated Him wrongly.*

He urged us to turn the other cheek to wrongdoers, give to those who rob us, and go the second mile with those who impose on our kindness (Matt. 5:38-46).

14. *Jesus did not need to make a name for himself.*

He preached, taught, and healed in the midst of all who came to Him, but He never attempted to create fame or fortune for himself as an outgrowth of His successful ministry (12:11-16). In fact, He actually sought to keep His popularity from growing (16:20).

15. *Jesus expressed strong emotion and indignation when the occasion called for it.*

Jesus did not get angry over selfish concerns or become self-defensive over personal attacks, but He did react strongly at times. For example, He created quite a scene in the Temple area over the money changers and dove sellers (21:12-13). He also became upset when His disciples tried to keep children away from His ministry (Mark 10:13-16).

16. *Jesus showed great courage throughout His life.*

He faced Satan's frontal attacks during 40 days of temptation. He courageously began His public ministry in the shadow of His popular cousin John's ministry. He publicly opposed the traditional laws that were inhumane and ungodly. He countered the religious leaders in their errors. He called sin by its real name and pointed to it in others' lives. He refused to lower himself to the demands of the people to crown Him as their king. He courageously accepted the Father's plan for His life even though it meant going to the Cross.

17. *Jesus had a clear mission and purpose for His life.*

He never surrendered to the immediate at the expense of the eternal.

This mission and purpose was clearly in place by the time He first visited the Temple at age 12 (Luke 2:49). He carried this vision with Him throughout His earthly ministry (4:18). He worked daily with a sense of urgency. He envisioned the harvest of souls at hand and did all He could to bring that harvest to His Father (John 4:34-38).

18. *Jesus lived with eternity's values in view.*

Jesus kept His feet firmly planted on the ground, so to speak, but He never lost sight of heaven's view. Every event in His earthly life, from the beginning of His ministry to the Cross, gave Him opportunity to show how to respond in light of eternity's value system. He never surrendered to the immediate at the expense of the eternal. Every word He said, every miracle He performed all somehow related to God's eternal purposes. He maintained a strong patriotism toward the homeland of His true citizenship—the kingdom of God.

19. *Jesus realized and accepted His human limitations.*

When His body grew weary, He stopped and rested. He slept after difficult days of ministry. When His nervous system reached a point of exhaustion from the press of the crowds, He withdrew from society and spent time alone. When He saw His ministry growing, He delegated tasks to His disciples rather than trying to do everything himself. When the burden grew heavy in the Garden of Gethsemane, He sought His disciples' help in carrying the load.

20. *Jesus always sought to do His Father's will.*

He demonstrated this perspective at age 12 (Luke 2:49) and carried it with Him to the Garden of Gethsemane (Matt. 26:39, 42). His life was driven by obedience to the Father's work and plan. More than anything, He wanted to see His Father's will accomplished (John 4:34; 6:38). In everything He did, Jesus saw himself as an ambassador for the Father.

21. *Jesus lived in constant communion with His Father.*

Prayer remained a constant source of strength for Jesus. He bathed the beginning of His ministry in prayer (Luke 6:12). He spent extended seasons of prayer after particularly taxing events, such as the feeding of the thousands (Mark 6:46). He called attention to the importance of prayer before performing miracles (John 11:41-42).

22. *Jesus depended on the Holy Spirit for constant spiritual strength and encouragement.*

The Spirit filled Jesus to adequately prepare Him for His battle with Satan's temptations (Luke 4:1-2). Everything Jesus accomplished in His earthly life He accomplished through the power of God's Spirit working through Him. This became clear as He came to the end of His life on earth and prayed that His disciples and those of us who would believe later might have that same Spirit working in them (John 17:1-26). William Blake reminds, "No bird soars too high if he soars with his own wings."[2]

23. *Jesus lived a life of service.*

Whether ministering to the multitudes, the 70 close followers, or the 12 disciples, Jesus found ways to give himself away in service to those who needed Him. He placed their needs ahead of His own needs. He left us an admonition to selfless service in the parable of the sheep and the goats. The focal point of that story rings in our ears to this day, "The King will reply, 'I tell you the truth, whatever you did for one of the least of these brothers of mine, you did for me'" (Matt. 25:40). After washing His disciples' feet, Jesus said, "I have set you an example that you should do as I have done for you" (John 13:15).

24. *Jesus submitted himself to suffering on our behalf.*

Jesus' sufferings are clearly documented throughout the New Testament Gospels. Paul reminds us of our part in sharing this ministry of suffering. "For just as the sufferings of Christ flow over into our lives, so also through Christ our comfort overflows" (2 Cor. 1:5). Paul's heart cried out to participate with Christ in this way. "I want to know Christ and the power of his resurrection and the fellowship of sharing his sufferings, becoming like him in his death" (Phil. 3:10). Peter also realized the need for us to follow Christ's example. "To this you were called, because Christ suffered for you, leaving you an example, that you should follow in his steps" (1 Pet. 2:21).

25. *Jesus submitted himself to death on the Cross to accomplish our salvation.*

Christ's death on the Cross opened the way for us to live in vital relationship with the Father. It also led to the formation of the Church, the Body of Christ on earth, which carries on His work until He returns.

Christ's crucifixion symbolizes the importance of our own daily crucifixion to self-will and self-denial (Gal. 2:20). Further, it reminds us that if we live and witness for Christ, we will pay the price along with Him.

> ### If we live and witness for Christ, we will pay the price along with Him.

"Now I rejoice in what was suffered for you, and I fill up in my flesh what is still lacking in regard to Christ's afflictions, for the sake of his body, which is the church" (Col. 1:24). We must always remember Jesus' words to His disciples, "If anyone would come after me, he must deny himself and take up his cross and follow me" (Matt. 16:24).

This list in no way exhausts the many aspects of Christlikeness we can emulate. We could also consider such things as patience, sympathy, frankness, cooperation, discernment of truth, nonconformity, reconciliation, and peace. Peter and Paul each list Christian virtues, which we should seek in our lives. Peter reminds us of these virtues: "For this very reason, make every effort to add to your faith goodness; and to goodness, knowledge; and to knowledge, self-control; and to self-control, perseverance; and to perseverance, godliness; and to godliness, brotherly kindness; and to brotherly kindness, love" (2 Pet. 1:5-7). Paul reminds: "Not only so, but we also rejoice in our sufferings, because we know that suffering produces perseverance; perseverance, character; and character, hope. And hope does not disappoint us, because God has poured out his love into our hearts by the Holy Spirit, whom he has given us" (Rom. 5:3-5).

The Challenge

"Let us fix our eyes on Jesus, the author and perfecter of our faith, who for the joy set before him endured the cross, scorning its shame, and sat down at the right hand of the throne of God" (Heb. 12:2). That's our challenge. We don't look in the mirror each morning and decide which Christlike virtues we'll strive for today. We do not have the strength and ability to do it even if we wanted to. Rather, we fix our eyes on Jesus and depend on His Holy Spirit to work His transforming miracle through us, as we remain open to His work in our lives.

Then we face the world; we don't withdraw from it. Instead, we go to work or school every day and serve as salt, light, and yeast in a spiritually darkened environment. We live as His ambassadors representing God's holy kingdom. We willingly suffer when we're called upon to suffer, and we serve whenever we can find avenues of service. We give Him all of the glory for every good thing accomplished in us. Each day we seek, as John says, to "walk as Jesus did" (1 John 2:6).

Charles M. Sheldon wrote one of the most popular Christian books of the 19th century, titled *In His Steps*. In it he posed a series of hypothetical challenges and then asked what Jesus would do in each of these settings. The book challenged readers to realize the importance of representing Jesus in daily activity. This book's intent remains popular today through WWJD? jewelry and notions.

We should answer that question, "What would Jesus do?" in our daily lives. As we put our answer into practice, we become more like Christ. As we become more like Christ, we bring a big smile to our Heavenly Father's face. I can almost hear Him say, "I love it when a plan comes together!" What a picture! A Father as proud of His children as He was the first time He held them in His arms in the garden. What an incredible love! What an adventure story!

NOTES

Chapter 1

1. Evan Esar, *20,000 Quips and Quotes* (New York: Barnes and Noble Books, 1968), 574.

Chapter 2

1. Billy Hughey and Joyce Hughey, *A Rainbow of Hope* (El Reno, Okla.: Rainbow Studies, 1994), 140.
2. Ibid., 128.
3. Stevens W. Anderson, *Compact Classics,* Vol. 3 (Salt Lake City, Utah: Lan C. England, 1994), 439.

Chapter 4

1. Eleanor Doan, *The Complete Speaker's Sourcebook,* Vol. 1 (Grand Rapids, Mich.: Zondervan Publishing House, 1996), 68.
2. Ortho Jennings, "Areas of Growth After Sanctification," in Kenneth Geiger, *Further Insights into Holiness* (Kansas City: Beacon Hill Press, 1963), 154.
3. Hughey and Hughey, *Rainbow of Hope,* 132.
4. John Wesley, *The Works of John Wesley,* 3rd ed., 14 vols. (Reprint, Kansas City: Beacon Hill Press of Kansas City, 1978-79), 6:65.

Chapter 6

1. Anderson, *Compact Classics,* Vol. 3, 431.
2. Ibid., 432.
3. Doan, *Complete Speaker's Sourcebook,* Vol. 2, 103.

Chapter 7

1. Hughey and Hughey, *Rainbow of Hope,* 23.
2. Wesley, *Works,* 2:372.

Chapter 8

1. Mother Teresa, *Total Surrender,* ed. Brother Angelo Devananda (Ann Arbor, Mich.: Servant Publications, 1985), 63.
2. Anderson, *Compact Classics,* Vol. 3, 443.
3. Stevens W. Anderson, *Compact Classics,* Vol. 1 (Salt Lake City: Lan C. England, 1991), 183.

Chapter 9

1. John Wesley, *A Plain Account of Christian Perfection* (Kansas City: Beacon Hill Press of Kansas City, 1966), 12.
2. Hughey and Hughey, *Rainbow of Hope,* 40.
3. Anderson, *Compact Classics,* Vol. 3, 44.
4. Anderson, *Compact Classics,* Vol. 1, 184.
5. Ibid., 185.
6. Ibid., 121.
7. Hughey and Hughey, *Rainbow of Hope,* 179.

8. Jennings, "Areas of Growth After Sanctification," 159-60.

9. Mother Teresa, *Total Surrender,* 31.

10. Jennings, "Areas of Growth After Sanctification," 154.

Chapter 10

1. Esar, *20,000 Quips and Quotes,* 16.

2. Anderson, *Compact Classics,* Vol. 3, 434.

3. Ibid., 433.

4. Anderson, *Compact Classics,* Vol. 1, 165.

5. Ibid., 168.

Chapter 11

1. Doan, *Complete Speaker's Sourcebook,* Vol. 2, 205.

2. Hughey and Hughey, *Rainbow of Hope,* 72.

3. Ibid., 141.

4. Anderson, *Compact Classics,* Vol. 2, 506.

5. Mother Teresa, *Total Surrender,* 73.

6. Ayn Rand, *The Virtue of Selfishness* (New York: Penguin Books USA, Inc., 1964).

7. Hughey and Hughey, *Rainbow of Hope,* 40.

8. Ibid., 61.

9. Anderson, *Compact Classics,* Vol. 1, 186.

10. Doan, *Complete Speaker's Sourcebook,* Vol. 2, 205.

Chapter 12

1. Ibid., 68.

Chapter 13

1. Ibid., 79.

2. Hughey and Hughey, *Rainbow of Hope,* 117.

not used